D0528564

MODERN BALLROOM DANCING

THEORY AND TECHNIQUE

OF

BALLROOM DANCING

By
VICTOR SILVESTER
The World's Greatest Authority on Ballroom Dancing

3/6 net.

MR. & MRS. VICTOR SILVESTER

The World-famous exponents of Ballroom Dancing

Victor Silvester is Vice-President of the Ballroom Branch, I.S.T.D.
Winners of the World's Dancing Championship, and leader of the Ballroom
Orchestra under his name which records exclusively for the Parlophone Company

MODERN BALLROOM DANCING

BY

VICTOR SILVESTER

Winner of the World's Dancing Championship

Vice-President of the Ballroom Branch of the Imperial Society of Teachers of Dancing

Leader of the Victor Silvester Ballroom Orchestra which records exclusively for the Parlophone Company and broadcasts regularly for the B.B.C.

1940

EDITION

HERBERT JENKINS LIMITED
3 DUKE OF YORK STREET
ST. JAMES'S, LONDON, S.W.1

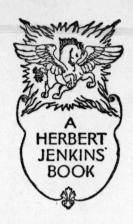

A
HERBERT
JENKINS'
BOOK

1st	Printing	January 1927
2nd	,,	September 1930
3rd	,,	January 1932
4th	,,	October 1932
5th	,,	March 1933
6th	,,	January 1934
7th	,,	February 1934
8th	,,	January 1935
9th	,,	April 1935
10th	,,	January 1936
11th	,,	February 1936
12th	,,	April 1936
13th	,,	January 1937
14th	,,	February 1937
15th	,,	May 1937
16th	,,	December 1937
17th	,,	January 1938
18th	,,	March 1938
19th	,,	October 1938
20th	,,	January 1939
21st	,,	May 1939
22nd	,,	November 1939
23rd	,,	February 1940
24th	,,	April 1940

MADE AND PRINTED IN GREAT BRITAIN BY
EBENEZER BAYLIS AND SON, LTD., THE
TRINITY PRESS, WORCESTER, AND LONDON

"What is a fine person or a beauteous face,
  Unless deportment give them decent grace;
  Blessed with all other requisites to please,
  To want the striking elegance of ease;
  Awkward, embarrassed, stiff, without the skill
  Of moving gracefully, or standing still."

CHURCHILL.

WORLD-WIDE COMMENDATION

THE German translation of Victor Silvester's splendid book has already appeared in the second edition. Every teacher of Ballroom Dancing in Germany, as well as all good dancers who are interested in the best style have found this book to be indispensable.

Germany has made great progress in Ballroom Dancing and is one of the best dancing nations. In the big competitions and championships, the leading German couples, both amateur and professional, have given their exemplary British colleagues, the hardest, but at the same time the most fascinating, fights.

It is to the merit of Victor Silvester that he has helped in the most decisive manner to raise the standard of dancing in Germany. He has explained to all and demonstrated the perfection that can be attained in modern ballroom dancing. For those who are fond of knowledge, he has written the most intelligible, clear and solid book, that it is possible to write.

J. Lewitan.

Editor of the German dance magazine Der Tanz.

It gives me great pleasure to write about Victor
Silvester's book which is both practical and
detailed, and consequently of great importance
as an aid to attaining the highest standard of
ballroom dancing, which the Danish Society
"Danse-Ringen", has always been adherent to.
Because of this, Victor Silvester's book is much
used here in Denmark.

There are plenty of dancing descriptions, in
which a swarm of terms are used and the theme
so mixed, as to make them nearly worthless, but
the form which Victor Silvester makes use of, is
so practical and well utilized, that it has only
one fault—you can do without the dancing-
master!

Karl Merrild.
President of the Danish
Society "Danse-Ringen."

It is with very great pleasure that I write to
give my opinion of the books and teaching of
Mr. Victor Silvester.

Mr. Silvester has been to Holland on four
occasions, to give instruction at the Conferences
of the Nederl. Vereeniging van Dansleeraren
(Dutch Association of Teachers of Dancing)
and his instruction was not only of great
assistance to the members but also to everyone
interested in ballroom dancing in this country.

After Victor Silvester had been here, the
standard of dancing and teaching became much
higher than ever before, and he did more to
raise the standard than anyone before him. The

profession in this country are full of admiration
for his ability as a dancer and a teacher.

With reference to Mr. Silvester's books, I
should only like to say this—They are worth as
many pounds as they cost shillings. The books
are very helpful and wonderfully clear, and, in
my opinion, it is essential that every teacher of
Ballroom Dancing should have them.

Mr. Richardson of the "Dancing Times" says
that Mr. Silvester is an artist. In my opinion
he is the finest instructor of ballroom dancing in
the world, and also the best writer on the subject.

H. Kwekkeboom.
President of the N.V.V.D.

In Japan, Victor Silvester's books and articles in
the "Dancing Times", have effected a great deal
of influence upon us. Our Ballroom Dancing is
steadily taking after the English style, which is
upheld by him. I believe that very soon, Victor
Silvester's style will rule our whole dancing
circle, in which his name is famous.

Hyojiro Kato.
Manager of the
Takarazuka Kaikan.

CONTENTS

ILLUSTRATIONS

Modern Ballroom Dancing

ON DANCING

BALLROOM Dancing is the most popular pastime in the world. There has been no more striking development in social habits since the war than the rise of dancing to universal popularity. It is enjoyed by every class of the community and it is indulged in in all climates and weathers, no matter whether it be winter or summer, hot or cold, wet or fine.

Dancing is the biggest social asset you can equip yourself with to-day. It leads you to hours of enjoyment where you will have every opportunity of meeting other people. It will take your mind off your troubles and worries. It will offer you the chance of putting on your best clothes and stepping forth into a gay colourful background. That, as any mind doctor will tell you, is a mental tonic.

As an exercise, and for slimming, it is one of the healthiest in the world. It will give you mental poise, physical grace and fitness, apart from the pleasure you will derive from it. And rhythm is a prime essential to life.

There are still numerous people who hesitate about learning to dance. They seem to imagine they will have to master masses of intricate steps. They look upon dancing as the acquisition of a set of tricks. Nothing could be farther from the truth. The whole point about modern ballroom dancing is that it is built up on natural foundations. Its basis is the walk. If you can walk well to music with good style and movement—you can dance.

Good dancing, like every other sport or pastime, is a question of balance. Balance is the correct carriage of the weight of your body, and I ask my readers to pay particular attention to the chapter on this subject. It is the all-important factor, the fundamental principle of ballroom dancing.

There is no prancing on tiptoe to-day. The good dancers glide in a smooth, silky style, effortless and simple. Dancing is "streamlined". Yet it is so easy to learn, providing you are taught correctly in the first place.

The idea is still prevalent that dancing is always changing, that one no sooner learns a few steps than they are old-fashioned. Well, let me contradict that fallacy once and for all. Dancing is not doing numerous steps and being thoroughly up-to-date. It is possible to know the latest steps and yet be a shocking dancer. To dance well is to move well, to have balance and style, to use your body, legs and feet correctly, heel and toe in the right place; to have rhythm, and to keep your muscles controlled and relaxed: to let your legs swing from the hips like pendulums, and to make everything look easy and effortless. *That* is dancing. It is not *What* you dance, it is *How* you dance that matters.

Dance-teaching to-day is standardized. This means that wherever you learn to dance in Britain, on the Continent, in the Colonies, or as far afield as Japan—if you go to recognized teachers who are qualified—you will receive the same basic instruction. No longer does every teacher or school have their own steps, and technique. Every good teacher sets out to teach you good style, balance and movement. No trick figures or stunts, freak dances or odd styles. Like tennis, football, cricket, golf or any other sport you like to name, there is a reason for everything you do: movements are not a passing fashion or the current whim of any teacher. The basic principles are fundamental and cannot be changed. They are as permanent as the law of gravity.

There are of course, always advanced variations that the good and enthusiastic dance fan can add to his repertoire, but the basis is always the same.

To-day there are four standard dances. In ten years time they will be exactly the same. They are the Quickstep, Slow Foxtrot, Waltz and Tango.

My advice to beginners is to master the elementary figures of the Quickstep and Waltz. Learn to do them with ease, good style and balance, then you will have something that will last you a lifetime.

The English style (as it is known on the Continent) has been copied and taught by practically every good dance teacher throughout the world because it is admittedly the best. This book will guide you along the right lines to acquiring it. Afterwards go to a good teacher to consolidate what you have learnt from these pages.

THE GENTLEMAN'S HOLD FOR ALL THE MODERN BALLROOM DANCES
(*See illustration.*)

STAND in a perfectly natural and erect position, head naturally poised. Raise the left arm so that the hand is slightly above the level of the left shoulder: bend the arm at the elbow so as to effect a graceful and easy curve. The left hand should grasp the lady's right hand so that it lies in his, with the palm of her hand downwards. The right hand should be just under the lady's left shoulder-blade. Both elbows should be kept well up, without of course raising the shoulders. Remember to keep the left forearm, wrist and hand in a straight line.

Hold your partner directly in front of you, or as near to directly in front as to be compatible with your comfort. In Tango you should hold your partner slightly more on one side (on your right hip).

Steer and control your partner with your body and right hand—not with your left. The left hand is held up for balancing purposes and appearance, not for leading your partner with.

In the Tango, the left forearm is bent inwards more, so that the hand is held closer to the head. Also the right arm should be placed further round your partner so that your right hand is underneath her right shoulder-blade.

Photo by Tunbridge

THE HOLD
For Lady and Gentleman

THE LADY'S HOLD FOR ALL THE MODERN BALLROOM DANCES
(*See illustration.*)

STAND in a perfectly natural and erect position, head naturally poised, looking over your partner's right shoulder. Raise the right hand to the same level as your partner's, keeping the palm of the hand downwards. The right arm should be bent slightly at the elbow. Raise the left arm and place the hand with the fingers close together, on the back of the man's right upper-arm. Both elbows should be kept well up, without of course raising the shoulders.

Never attempt in any way to lead or guide your partner, submit yourself entirely to him. Do not lean on him or anticipate what is coming next, just follow.

IMPORTANT POINTS TO REMEMBER

1.—Relax all your muscles: don't keep them taut.
2.—Don't hunch your shoulders or move your arms about, keep them perfectly still.
3.—Keep your knees straight when you are out to the full extent of your stride. Apart from this they should be naturally relaxed the whole time. Stiff knees and bent knees look frightfully ugly: try to strike the happy medium.
4.—Don't hold your breath, breathe naturally.
5.—Use your heels whenever it feels comfortable and natural to do so. This will improve your balance, carriage and movement, and looks much better than being perched up on your toes the whole time. In some steps you put the heel down first, others the flat foot, and some toes first. (These I have described.) Practice and lessons from a competent teacher will put you right.
6.—Always dance in time to the music, never out of time.
7.—Don't turn your toes out, your feet should be perfectly straight.
8.—Take long steps straight from the hips: not too long, just the length of your natural

stride, and skim your feet along the floor, in every dance except the Tango, where the feet are picked up slightly.

9.—Always keep your legs close together when one foot passes the other: nothing looks worse than to see a person dancing with legs apart.

10.—Be perfectly natural, don't try and ape someone else or get an affected hold, people only laugh at you.

11.—When you dance look as though you are enjoying it.

12.—If you want to talk, sit out.

13.—BALANCE. (Very important. See chapter on this subject.) WHEN MOVING FORWARD (lady or gentleman) THE WEIGHT OF YOUR BODY SHOULD ALWAYS BE FORWARD. Do not push your foot out in front of you leaving the weight of your body back. If you do you will tread on your partner's toes.

WHEN MOVING BACKWARD (lady or gentleman) THE WEIGHT OF YOUR BODY SHOULD ALWAYS BE FORWARD. To prevent your weight from being carried back, swing your leg well back from the hip and DO NOT LOWER YOUR BACK HEEL UNTIL THE OTHER FOOT PASSES IT.

It is essential that you should master this thoroughly before attempting to learn a single step, if you wish to dance well and make it a pleasure for your partners as well as for yourself.

Remember that whichever direction

you move in—forwards, backwards, sideways, turning—the weight of your body
must be forward—towards your partner
without leaning forwards.

14.—Use as few walking steps as possible in
between the different figures which you
learn. Try and amalgamate them where
possible by making the last step of one
figure the first step of the next figure. (See
How to Construct the Dances.)

BALANCE

(See illustration.)

Good balance is the greatest essential to the
making of a good dancer. Balance means the
correct carriage of the weight of the body when
moving backwards and forwards. If you can
walk backwards and forwards with a partner
and carry your weight in the correct place, it
will not take you very long to dance well, but
of course, to obtain good balance is a matter of
practice. Your legs must swing freely from the
hips and at the same time your body must remain naturally erect and upright.

The rule to remember is that the weight of
your body (lady or gentleman) should always
be forward, towards your partner, in whatever
direction you are moving. This does not mean
to say that you must lean forward. As I have
just stated, you must remain naturally erect.

Here is a little suggestion: when dancing
think of yourself (lady or gentleman) as trying

BALANCE

The greatest essential to the making of a good dancer
Note how the weight of the body is forward, both for the lady and for the gentleman

gently to push your partner over, when you are moving forward: and trying to stop your partner from coming forward, when you are moving backwards. Do not, of course, try any drastic pushing, but just keep that idea at the back of your mind: it will demonstrate where the weight of your body should be. If at any moment your legs were suddenly knocked from under you, you should fall on to your face and not on to the back of your head!

Now let us think of it from the point of view of the legs or feet.

As you go to take a walk forward, your weight must of course, be on the back foot, but remember to release the heel of this back foot so that your weight is carried in a forward direction. When you are out to the full extent of your stride, you should be on the heel of your front foot and the ball of your back foot, your weight being central—evenly divided between both feet. A fraction of a second afterwards you should lower on to the flat of your front foot transferring your weight on to it. As you do this your back foot should be on the toes before it is released to move forwards.

Now to take a walk backwards. Swing your leg well back from the hip going on to the toes of the foot first: this latter point is most important. You must use your ankle and go on to the toes first—not the ball of the foot. As you take this step back, your weight must of course, be on your front foot. As you continue, your weight becomes central by lowering on to the ball of your back foot (not the heel) and allowing the toes of your front foot to leave the floor slightly. (You will now be supported by the ball of your back foot and the heel of your front foot.) Your weight should now be transferred on to the ball of your back foot and the front foot should be pulled back with pressure on the heel. Your back heel should not be allowed to touch the floor until the other foot passes it. This latter point is of the utmost importance and it applies in every ballroom dance when you are moving backwards. If you lower your back heel too soon, the whole weight of your body is carried backward, thereby pulling your partner forward making it look most ungainly, and uncomfortable for you both.

In brief, when moving forwards, your weight must be on the back foot—central—front foot, and when moving backwards, it must be on the front foot—central—back foot.

CONTRARY BODY MOVEMENT

For any dancer who wishes to attain the highest standard in the ballroom, it is necessary to have a thorough knowledge, both in theory and practice, of what is known as contrary body movement.

To teach this to a beginner is futile: it cannot be learnt in a few lessons, and it is ridiculous to attempt it. It is reserved solely for those who have acquired good balance and movement. For a professional it is an essential of the utmost importance.

To put it briefly, contrary body movement

makes the difference between a straight line and a curve. In ballroom dancing these curves are obtained by turning your body slightly so that the opposite hip and shoulder are towards the leg that you are stepping with.

The four ways that contrary body movement can be used are as follows:—

Step forward with the R.F. turning your L. hip and shoulder forward.

Step forward with the L.F. turning your R. hip and shoulder forward.

Step back with the R.F. turning the L. hip and shoulder backward.

Step back with the L.F. turning the R. hip and shoulder backward.

This movement is always initiated in the shoulders and carried down to the hips.

Contrary movement must not be used indiscriminately, it is only used at certain times and in certain places, and I have mentioned where it should be used in my descriptions of the different steps. It is used on practically every turning step.

It is important to remember that the opposite hip and shoulder should turn as you take your step, not after you have taken it.

When this movement is introduced on a step, your body will face a certain direction. You must continue to face that direction, more or less, on all the following steps, until the next one on which you use contrary movement again.

There is another form of contrary body movement, known as contrary body movement position, which occurs when taking a step across

your body. If you take a step forward with
your R.F. across to your left, keeping your body
facing your front, it will be noticed that you get
the same effect as if you stepped straight forward with your R.F. at the same time turning
your L. hip and shoulder forward.

This second form of contrary movement—
contrary body movement position—is used on
all "outside" steps; that is, on any variation
where you step outside your partner or your
partner steps outside you. It is also used very
much in the Tango, and it occurs on other steps
in ballroom dancing.

The border line between contrary body movement and contrary body movement position is
sometimes so slight that it is difficult to differen-
tiate between the two.

Another very important point to remember in
both forms of contrary movement is that it must
be used by the entire body from the feet upwards. The commonest fault is for a person to
break at the waist, turning the shoulders only.
The entire trunk of the body must always turn
in one piece without any break in the middle—
at the waist.

Another useful hint is to allow your back foot
to turn inwards ever so slightly, when using
contrary movement. Actually it is only pointing
the way that you are facing but if you *think*
of it as being turned inwards slightly, it will help
you no end. The tendency with most people is
to turn the back foot outwards. Doing this pulls
on the hip muscles and prevents the hips from
turning with the shoulders.

Body Sway

This subject, although not so important as Balance and Contrary Body Movement, is nevertheless a very great asset towards the finished article. It should never be attempted by anyone but an experienced dancer. This slight sway of the body is introduced into the majority of turning steps in ballroom dancing, in order to help you to retain good balance, and the inclination of the body should always be towards the centre of the turn that you are making. It also occurs on certain other figures apart from turns.

In a ballroom you always dance round it anti-clockwise, and there are only two basic ways that you can turn, natural (right-handed) or reverse (left-handed). If you think this over for a few minutes, you will appreciate therefore, that with a natural turn you always sway slightly towards the middle of the ballroom, and with a reverse turn you always sway slightly towards the outside of the ballroom—the wall.

Another and perhaps easier way of thinking of this is as follows:—

For the Slow Foxtrot and Quickstep—

If you have taken a "slow" step forwards or backwards with your R.F. then you sway to the right on the two "quick" steps following.

If you have taken a "slow" step forwards or backwards with your L.F. then you sway to the left on the two " quick" steps following.

For the Waltz.—

If you have taken the " 1 " forwards or backwards with your R.F. then you sway to the right for the "2, 3."

If you have taken the "1" forwards or backwards with your L.F. then you sway to the left for the "2, 3."

In the Tango there is no body sway at all.

The sway when introduced should be carried from the feet upwards, so that the whole of your body—legs, hips, shoulders, and head—is inclined towards the centre of the turn that you are making. If a straight line were drawn through your body as this slight sway was introduced, it should divide you equally into two parts so that no one part should overlap.

You must not sway over from the waist.

This sway may be likened to a runner taking a curve on the track, he will naturally sway towards the centre of the track. The same with a cyclist taking a corner, or an aeroplane banking.

Do not forget that the sway must be very slight, and should you have any doubt whatsoever, as to which way you should incline, leave it out altogether until you can get a professional to explain it to you.

Remember, under no circumstances attempt this unless you are thoroughly experienced and have mastered balance, and contrary body movement and can construct your dances without any difficulty.

Rise and Fall

In Ballroom Dancing it is necessary to introduce what is known as rise and fall. The reasons for this I will explain. Dancing is, what one might term, a cross between running and walking. When you run you use the balls of the feet; when you walk—the heels. In every dance with the exception of the Waltz, the different figures are made up of slow steps and quick steps. The slow steps can be looked upon as walking steps and the quick ones as running steps, therefore it follows that there will be a rise on to the balls of the feet on the quick steps. There are of course, exceptions, but as a general rule the above applies. It is not, however, applicable to the Tango, because in this dance there is no rise and fall whatsoever, every step, no matter whether it be quick or slow is taken after the manner of walking.

The rise and fall is given underneath the description of each figure. They have been worked out to a nicety and the reader should remember that, as with everything in ballroom dancing, the rise and fall given is the most natural and comfortable method of obtaining a smooth, gliding movement.

Every rise and fall should be gradual and soft, not sharp and jerky.

MUSCLE CONTROL

You will all have noticed in the ballroom certain couples who move their arms about when dancing. This shows lack of muscle control in its most crude form. It is usually known as "pump-handling". These people do not do it intentionally, they simply cannot move their legs without moving their arms.

The body should always be kept quite still: not stiff and rigid, but relaxed and controlled, and you should only move from the hips as you take your steps. To obtain perfect muscle control is a matter of practice. As in every form of exercise, one desires to get the maximum effect, both in pleasure and health, with the minimum amount of effort, and it takes a little time and perseverance to do this.

STEERING

This rests solely with the man, and it is his duty to follow the course of the ballroom, the line of dance, without making himself a nuisance to other dancers. He may, of course, move for two or three steps against the line of dance but only if there is no one in his way.

POSITION

Keep your partner in front of you, except in the Tango where your partner is slightly on one side (on your right hip). This is sometimes rather difficult if your partner happens to be nearly as tall as you are, for it is impossible for you to see where you are steering. Under such circumstances, it is better to hold your partner slightly to your right, on your right hip, but do not do this if it can be avoided.

The position of the partners to each other should be close, so that both move as one person. If you look at the perfect dancing couple in profile, no space will be visible between them.

FEET

For ballroom dancing your feet should be kept perfectly straight. There is nothing that looks so hideous or ungainly than to see someone dancing with their feet turned out. Your feet should be used in the same manner as when walking in the street, that is they should be dead straight. I would advise all readers to pay particular attention to their walk, apart from dancing. Their whole appearance will improve if they counteract the tendency to turn the feet outwards.

In every dance except the Tango, some part of your foot—heel, flat foot, ball of foot or toes—should remain in contact with the floor throughout the entire dance. If you do this, using your feet correctly and keeping your weight in the right place, it will give you a smooth, gliding movement, instead of an otherwise bumpy and ungainly one.

The footwork of a good dancer is beautiful to watch and it is only obtained by using the heel, flat foot, ball of foot and toes, at the right moment in the right place.

ANKLES AND INSTEPS

The muscles in the ankles and insteps should be supple and pliable. The majority of people do not use their ankles at all. If they are not used correctly they can upset the whole balance of your body. As an instance, when you step backward you should use your ankle so that you stretch back on to the toes of your foot. If you only go back on to the ball of the foot it will shorten your stride by four or five inches. Try this and see.

Also when moving forward you should make sure, before releasing your back foot that you have allowed it to go right on to the toes by using your ankle and instep correctly.

This will make a world of difference to your dancing if put into practice. Should your ankle and instep muscles be stiff through disuse, it will of course, take a little exercise and practice to loosen them up.

KNEES

If you watch a good couple dancing, you should never notice their knees. If you do notice them, you may be sure that there is something the matter which has drawn your attention to them: either they are too stiff or too bent. From the point of view of a spectator a dancer's knees should appear to be straight (not stiff, there's a great difference) but actually in practice the knees should always be naturally relaxed (not bent) throughout, with the one exception of when you are out to the full extent of your stride when taking a step. For the fraction of a second the knee of the leg that you are stepping with should be dead straight (not stiff). The moment afterwards as that same leg takes the weight of your body it should relax naturally.

Correct use of the knees marks the difference between a hard and a soft movement.

In Tango the knees are relaxed more, for the simple reason that your feet leave the floor ever so slightly. This stands to reason for if your foot is kept in contact with the floor it will keep your knees comparatively straight, whereas if it is lifted, be it ever so slight, the leg is bound to relax more at the knee.

Hips

To stretch from the hips when taking a step forwards or backwards is one of the hardest things to acquire in ballroom dancing. It is however, an essential to good dancing and it is certainly worth the perseverance and practice that is necessary in order to attain it.

A beginner will nearly always try to step from the knee or the waist, the latter by leaning forward and allowing his (or her) hips to fall away. The hips should be kept in or forward without giving the appearance of leaning backwards. Study the illustration of Balance and you will see where they should be. To get them in the right place keep them forward without allowing the shoulders to go back.

In order to stretch from the hips when taking a step it is again necessary to make sure that the feet, ankles and knees are being used correctly.

A fault in any one part of the anatomy can

cause half a dozen others. I would stress therefore, that however boring my readers may find it,
they should make a point of learning to walk
forwards and backwards with a partner until
they can do it with ease, comfort and good
balance. After that, dancing will be easy and a
real pleasure.

POISE

This is a fine point which effects the finesse of
one's dancing. Although the balance of the
body—the carriage of the weight—is exactly
the same for the lady as for the gentleman, the
poise of the body is slightly different. For the
man, his body should be poised slightly forward,
whilst for the lady, her body should be poised
slightly backward from the hips upward.
Remember not to confuse this with the balance
of the body.

TIME

It is necessary for every dancer to have some
idea of "time". In the following table I have
given the "time" that the music of each dance
is written in, i.e., the number of beats in each
bar. This is more for the professional than the
amateur dancer, but it is essential that everyone
should dance in time to the music. In all
dances, with the exception of the waltz, there
are two rhythms that one uses to dance to, the
slow and the quick. It is better to get someone
to explain this to you, should you not be sure.

Tempo

Tempo denotes the speed at which a dance is played, i.e., the number of bars to the minute. The correct tempo of each dance is given in the table on page 34.

Rhythm

Rhythm is the regular occurrence of an accentuated beat or beats in the music. It may also be referred to as the individual expression that a dancer puts into his or her steps. A man might dance in time to the music and yet have no rhythm. You could not have rhythm dancing out of time.

TABLE GIVING TIMES, TEMPI AND RHYTHMS
used in the standard ballroom dances.

NOTE.—As many dance bands play at varying tempi, I am giving in this table the ideal tempo for each dance and in brackets underneath the minimum and maximum tempi that it is possible to dance to. The ideal tempo allows for long, natural length strides. If, therefore, the bands play quicker than the ideal tempo, the dancer should shorten his steps proportionately, and if they play slower, then he should lengthen them in like manner.

DANCE	TIME	TEMPO	NO. OF RHYTHMS USED
Slow Foxtrot	4/4	32 bars per min. (28 to 36).	Two. Slow & Quick, Quick, Slow.
Quickstep	4/4	48 bars per min. (38 to 54).	Two. Slow & Quick, Quick, Slow.
Waltz	3/4	34 bars per min. (30 to 40).	One. (A step to each beat, except when hesitation steps are introduced.)
Tango	2/4	30 bars per min. (28 to 34).	Two. Slow & Quick, Quick, Slow.
Rumba	4/4	44 bars per min. (40 to 48).	Two. Slow, Quick, Quick, & Slow.
Waltz (quick) (Viennese waltz)	3/4	56 bars per min. (44 to 60)	Three. A step to each beat. Two steps to three beats. One step to three beats.

ABBREVIATIONS AND EXPLANATIONS

USED IN DIAGRAMS AND DESCRIPTION OF STEPS

R.—Right.

L.—Left.

R.F.—Right foot.

L.F.—Left foot.

S.—A slow step.

Q.—A quick step.

L.O.D.—The line of dance. (This means the direction that one takes when dancing round a ballroom. Anti-clock-wise.)

C.B.M.—Contrary body movement.

C.B.M.P.—Contrary body movement position.

P.P.—Promenade position. A position similar to that of the Promenade in the Tango, in which the partners open out fanwise to each other, the lady's left hip remaining in contact with the gentleman's right hip.

In the diagrams the right foot is illustrated thus—

and the left foot—

35

The dotted outline of the foot is the position of that foot after you have turned on it.

The above denotes a turn on the ball of the R.F. as it occurs in the diagrams given with each dance.

The above denotes a turn on the heel of the L.F.

In nearly all the figures of the different dances each foot is moved alternately, the same as when you walk, i.e., you take a step with the L.F. and then a step with the R.F. (or vice-versa.) In following the diagrams, it will help the reader a great deal if he or she remembers this point, for it will be noticed that in the numbering, 1, 3, 5, 7 will be, say, the L.F., therefore 2, 4, 6, 8 will be the R.F. (or vice-versa.)

You will find the diagrams easier to follow if you always face the direction in which the toes are pointing. As you turn, turn the diagram as well.

Let your feet follow along the lines in which the arrows are pointing.

The diagrams are not intended to be mathematically exact, but merely to show the pattern made in the different figures. The inside of the page on which each diagram is drawn represents the middle of the ballroom, whilst the outside of the page represents the outside—the wall. The top of the page is equivalent to the line of dance. From this the reader will be able to understand which way he, or she, should be facing on each step.

TERMS USED IN DESCRIBING THE DIRECTION OF STEPS

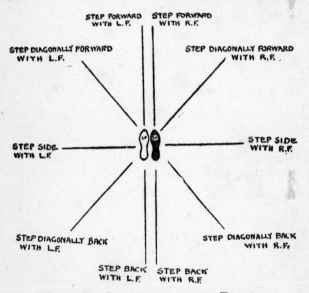

How to Construct the Dances

When you have mastered a few figures in a dance it is necessary to consider the best way to amalgamate them, or rather how to join them, one to the other.

The main point to remember in any dance is to avoid doing too many walks between each figure. When learning, it is certainly a good plan to begin with a few walks, do the figure you intend to, then do a few more walks before going into the next variation. This, however, should only be adhered to in the preliminary stages and as soon as you can perform the figures with a fair degree of accuracy you should attempt to join one on to the other, thereby eliminating the numerous walks that a beginner is apt to resort to whilst making up his mind what to do next.

The correct combination or sequences that you use is more a matter of practice and experience than anything else, but at the end of each dance I have given a description of the best variations to use after doing certain others.

You should aim to get a continuous flowing dance without any unnecessary breaks to spoil the continuity of your movement.

As far as possible try to follow a right-handed turn with a left-handed turn and vice-versa. Doing this will make a dance much more effective.

According to a dancer's ability and experience, so he can add other figures, but it is much better to make sure of the standardized figures and amalgamating them, before attempting anything more advanced.

THE SLOW FOXTROT

THIS dance, which might be rightly termed the English Foxtrot, has evolved from the chassé and chassé turns, into the three-step and "open" turns. The difference between the two is that in the former you closed your feet on the second step of each three, whereas in the latter you always pass them on the second step of each three.

The greater part of the technique of modern ballroom dancing has been formed out of this dance, and to anyone who is really a serious dancer or intends to take it up professionally, a thorough knowledge of the Slow Foxtrot is essential.

For the dancer who cannot give very much time to it, I would advise him to leave this dance and to begin with the most popular dance in the world to-day, the Quickstep.

The Slow Foxtrot is essentially a good dancer's dance, and its greatest handicap is that it requires a great deal of room to dance in comfort. It is very popular at the numerous dance halls throughout the country, owing to their spaciousness, but it is rarely seen in the smarter ballrooms of London as these are invariably small and crowded.

There are two fundamental steps in this dance, the Walk and the Three-step, and all the basic figures are made up of these two steps.

The Walk Forward

Take a long gliding step straight from the hips, skimming your foot lightly along the floor. When you are out to your full stretch you should be on the heel of your front foot: immediately lower on to the flat foot. Your back foot should now be on the toes before it is released to move forward. Repeat with the opposite leg. Each walk takes two beats of the music and is counted "slow". (For details of the carriage of weight in the Walk, see the chapter on Balance.) Keep moving forward continuously the whole time and do not release your back foot to move it forward until the last possible moment.

The Walk Backward

Swing your leg well back from the hip, going on to the toes first and keeping your weight on your front foot. As you continue, your weight should be carried between your feet, and the toes of your front foot should leave the floor so that the pressure is on the front heel. Your weight is then transferred on to the ball of the back foot, but your weight is still forward, as your back heel is off the floor. Continue and do not lower your back heel until the other foot passes it. Repeat with the opposite leg. Each walk takes two beats of the music and is counted "slow". (For fuller details, see the chapter on Balance.) With your weight forward, keep moving backward, continuously the whole time and do not release your front foot hurriedly: pull it back gradually with pressure on the heel.

THE THREE-STEP

A Three-step is really a running movement. It consists of three steps taken forwards or backwards, which are fitted to four beats of the music, and counted quick, quick, slow: the quick steps taking one beat each and the slow step two beats. The 1st step should be taken on the 1st beat, the 2nd step on the 2nd beat, the 3rd step on the 3rd beat and carried over the 4th beat. Each step should be long but the middle one (2nd) is a little shorter than the other two (1st and 3rd).

A three-step may either be R.F., L.F., R.F., or L.F., R.F., L.F.

In order to do the steps gracefully and with comfort, a rise and fall should be introduced. Rise up at the end of the 1st step and lower at the end of the 2nd step.

The Feather Step

GENTLEMAN

1. Long step forward with the R.F.   S.

Three-step
2. Step forward with the L.F. preparing to step outside your partner.   Q.
3. Step forward with the R.F. outside your partner.   Q.
4. Step forward with the L.F. in front of your partner.   S.

The rise on 2, 3, 4, is a little different from the ordinary three-step because you step outside your partner.

Rise and fall. Rise at the end of 1 and lower at the end of 3.

Contrary body movement. Used on 1 and 4. (C.B.M.P. on 3.)

Body sway. Sway slightly to the R. on 2 and 3.

The Feather Step

GENTLEMAN

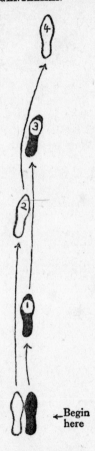

The Feather Step

LADY

	1.	Long step back with the L.F.	S.
Three-step {	2.	Step back with the R.F.	Q.
	3.	Step back with the L.F. (your partner steps outside).	Q.
	4.	Step back with the R.F.	S.

The rise on 2, 3, 4, is a little different from the ordinary three-step because your partner steps outside you.

Rise and fall. Rise at the end of 1 and lower at the end of 3.

Contrary body movement. Used on 1 and 4. (C.B.M.P. on 3.)

Body sway. Sway slightly to the L. on 2 and 3.

THE FEATHER STEP

LADY

THE NATURAL TURN

GENTLEMAN

1. Step forward with the R.F. turning on it to the R.   S.

Three-step
2. Step to the side with the L.F. still turning.   Q.
3. Step back with the R.F.   Q.
4. Step back with the L.F. turning on it to the R.   S.

5. Pull the R.F. back to the L.F. turning from the L. heel on to the R. heel (feet slighly apart).   S.
6. Step forward with the L.F.   S.

You should make just over three-quarters of a turn on the complete step.

Rise and fall. Rise at the end of 2 and lower at the end of 3.

Contrary body movement. Used on 1, 4, 6.

Body sway. Sway slightly to the R. on 2 and 3. Sway slightly to the L. on 5, holding it and straightening as weight goes on to 6.

The Natural Turn

GENTLEMAN

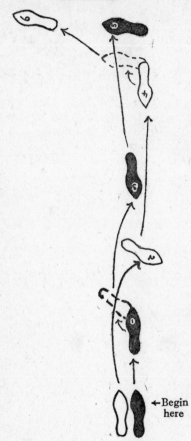

←Begin here

The Natural Turn

LADY

1. Step back with the L.F. turning on it to the R.   S.

Three-step
2. Close the R.F. back to the L.F. turning from the L. heel on to the R. heel (heel turn).   Q.
3. Step forward with the L.F.   Q.
4. Step forward with the R.F. turning on it to the R.   S.

5. Step to the side with the L.F.   S.
6. Brush the R.F. through (close to the L.F.) and step back with it.   S.

You should make just over three-quarters of a turn on the complete step.

Rise and fall. Rise at the end of 2 and lower at the end of 3.

Contrary body movement. Used on 1, 4, 6.

Body sway. Sway slightly to the L. on 2 and 3. Sway slightly to the R. on 5, holding it and straightening as weight goes on to 6.

THE NATURAL TURN

LADY

Begin here

The Reverse Turn

GENTLEMAN

1. Step forward with the L.F. turning on it to the L.   S.

Three-step
{
2. Step to the side with the R.F. still turning.   Q.
3. Step back with the L.F.   Q.
4. Step back with the R.F. turning on it to the L.   S.
}

Three-step
{
5. Step to the side with the L.F.   Q.
6. Step forward with the R.F. outside your partner.   Q.
7. Step forward with the L.F. in front of your partner.   S.
}

NOTE.—In practice, the Reverse Turn should be commenced facing diagonally to the middle of room. This makes it easier to do and is more natural and comfortable. It should be finished facing diagonally to the outside of the room.

You should make three-quarters of a turn on the complete figure.

Rise and fall. Rise at the end of 2 and lower at the end of 3. Rise again at the end of 4 and lower at the end of 6.

Contrary body movement. Used on 1, 4, 7. (C.B.M.P. on 6.)

Body sway. Sway slightly to the L. on 2 and 3, and slightly to the R. on 5 and 6.

The Reverse Turn

GENTLEMAN

The Reverse Turn

LADY

	1.	Step back with the R.F. turning on it to the L.	S.
Three-step	2.	Close the L.F. back to the R.F. turning from the R. heel on to the L. heel (heel turn).	Q.
	3.	Step forward with the R.F.	Q.
	4.	Step forward with the L.F. turning on it to the L.	S.
Three-step	5.	Step to the side with the R.F.	Q.
	6.	Step back with the L.F.	Q.
	7.	Step back with the R.F.	S.

You should make just over three-quarters of a turn on the complete step.

Rise and fall. Rise at the end of 2 and lower at the end of 3. Rise again at the end of 4 and lower at the end of 6.

Contrary body movement. Used on 1, 4, 7. (C.B.M.P. on 6.)

Body sway. Sway slightly to the L. on 2 and 3, and slightly to the L. on 5 and 6.

The Reverse Turn

LADY

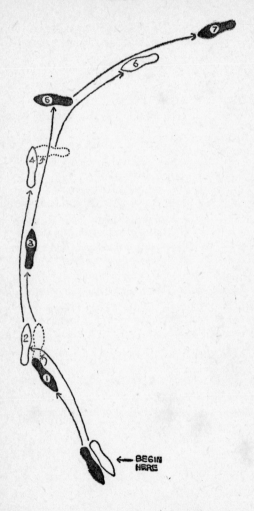

The Reverse Wave

GENTLEMAN

1. Step forward with the L.F. turning on it to the L. — S.

Three-step
2. Step to the side with the R.F. still turning. — Q.
3. Step back with the L.F. — Q.
4. Step back with the R.F. turning your body slightly (C.B.M.). — S.

Three-step
5. Step back with the L.F. — Q.
6. Step back with the R.F. — Q.
7. Step back with the L.F. turning on it to the R. — S.

8. Pull the R.F. back to the L.F. turning from the L. heel on to the R. heel (feet slightly apart). — S.
9. Step forward with the L.F. — S.

Make sure that the 4th step is taken with your back diagonally to the wall. It will be noticed that 1, 2, 3 are similar to 1,2, 3, of the Reverse Turn, and 6, 7, 8, 9, similar to 3, 4, 5, 6, of the Natural Turn.

Rise and fall. Rise at the end of 2 and lower at the end of 3. Rise again at the end of 5 and lower at the end of 6.

Contrary body movement. Used on 1, 4, 7, 9.

Body sway. Sway slightly to the L. on 2 and 3, and slightly to the R. on 5 and 6. Sway slightly to the L. on 8, holding it and straightening as weight goes on to 9.

THE REVERSE WAVE

GENTLEMAN

Begin
here

The Reverse Wave

LADY

	1.	Step back with the R.F. turning on it to the L.	S.
Three-step	2.	Close the L.F. back to the R.F. turning from the R. heel on to the L heel (heel turn).	Q.
	3.	Step forward with the R.F.	Q.
	4.	Step forward with the L.F. turning your body slightly (C.B.M.).	S.
Three-step	5.	Step forward with the R.F.	Q.
	6.	Step forward with the L.F.	Q.
	7.	Step forward with the R.F. turning on it to the R.	S.
	8.	Step to the side with the L.F.	S.
	9.	Brush the R.F. through (close to the L.F.) and step back with it.	S.

It will be noticed that 1, 2, 3, are similar to 1, 2, 3, of the Reverse Turn, and 6, 7, 8, 9, similar to 3, 4, 5, 6, of the Natural Turn.

Rise and fall. Rise at the end of 2 and lower at the end of 3. Rise again at the end of 5 and lower at the end of 6.

Contrary body movement. Used on 1, 4, 7, 9.

Body sway. Sway slightly to the R. on 2 and 3, and slightly to the L. on 5 and 6. Sway slightly to the R. on 8, holding it and straightening as weight goes on to 9.

THE REVERSE WAVE
LADY

Begin
here ←

The Change of Direction

This figure is used after the Feather Step, or preferably after the Reverse Turn, when at the end of the room—in a corner—or when you have not enough space to follow either of these figures with a three-step and Natural Turn.

GENTLEMAN

1. Step diagonally forward with the R.F. turning on it to the L.   S.
2. Brush the L.F. up to the R.F., relaxing both knees, and step forward with it.   S.

Make half a turn or less on this figure.

Rise and fall.   Nil.

Contrary body movement. Used on 2.

Body sway. Sway slightly to the L. on 1, holding it as L.F. is brushed through and straightening as weight goes on to 2.

LADY

1. Step diagonally back with the L.F. turning on it to the L.   S.
2. Brush the R.F. up to the L.F., relaxing both knees, and step back with it.   S.

Make half a turn or less on this figure.

Rise and fall.   Nil.

Contrary body movement. Used on 2.

Body sway. Sway slightly to the R. on 1, holding it as R.F. is brushed through and straightening as weight goes on to 2.

THE TELEMARK

GENTLEMAN

To go into the Telemark, do so after a Feather Step taken diagonally to the centre of room. Make the last step of the Feather Step the first of the Telemark. Make three-quarters of a turn to the L. on the complete figure, finishing it so that you are facing diagonally to the outside of room.

1. Step forward with the L.F. turning on it to the L.   S.
2. Step to the side with the R.F. still turning.   Q.
3. Short step to side with L.F. (facing wall).   Q.
4. Step forward with the R.F. outside partner,   S.
    and go straight into 2, 3, 4, of the Feather Step,
    or turn on 4 into 2, 3, 4, 5, 6, of the Natural Turn.

Rise and fall. Rise at the end of 2 and lower at the end of 3.

Contrary body movement. Used on 1 and 4.

Body sway. Sway slightly to the L. on 2 and 3.

LADY

1. Step back with the R.F. turning on it to the L.   S.
2. Close the L.F. back to the R.F. turning from R. heel on to L. heel (heel turn).   Q.
3. Step to the side with the R.F. (facing centre).   Q.
4. Step back with the L.F.   S.
    and go straight into 2, 3, 4, of the Feather Step,
    or turn on 4 into 2, 3, 4, 5, 6, of the Natural Turn.

Rise and fall. Rise at the end of 2 and lower at the end of 3.

Contrary body movement. Used on 1 and 4.

Body sway. Sway slightly to the R. on 2 and 3.

The Impetus Turn

GENTLEMAN

Do 1, 2, 3, of the Natural Turn, then

1. Step back with the L.F. turning on it to the R.   S.
2. Close the R.F. back to the L.F. (heel turn) making just over three-quarters of a turn to the R.   Q.
3. Short step diagonally back with the L.F.   Q.
4. Step back with the R.F. turning slightly to the L. and go straight into 5, 6, 7, of the Reverse Turn.   S.

Rise and fall. Rise at the end of 2 and lower at the end of 3.

Contrary body movement. Used on 1 and 4.

Body sway. Sway slightly to the L. on 2 and 3.

LADY

Do 1, 2, 3, of the Natural Turn, then

1. Step forward with the R.F. turning on it to the R.   S.
2. Short step to the side with L.F. still turning.   Q.
3. Brush R.F. up to L.F. and immediately take a short step diagonally forward with it.   Q.
4. Step forward with the L.F. turning slightly to the L. and go straight into 5, 6, 7, of the Reverse Turn.   S.

Rise and fall. Rise at the end of 2 and lower at the end of 3.

Contrary body movement. Used on 1 and 4.

Body sway. Sway slightly to R. on 2 and 3.

THE OPEN TELEMARK

To go into the Open Telemark, do so after a Feather Step taken diagonally to the centre of room. Make the last step of the Feather Step the first of the Open Telemark. Make three-quarters of a turn to the L. on the complete figure, finishing it so that you are facing diagonally to the outside of the room.

GENTLEMAN

1. Step forward with the L.F. turning on it to the L.   S.
2. Step to the side with the R.F. still turning.   Q.
3. Step to the side with the L.F. opening in to P.P. (facing wall).   Q.
4. Step through with the R.F. in P.P.   S.
   Then go straight into 2, 3, 4, of the Feather Step, or turn on 4 into 2, 3, 4, 5, 6, of Natural Turn.

Rise and fall. Rise at the end of 2 and lower at the end of 3.
Contrary body movement. Used on 1 and 4.
Body sway. Sway slightly to the L. on 2 and 3.

LADY

1. Step back with the R.F. turning on it to the L.   S.
2. Close the L.F. back to the R.F. turning from R. heel on to L. heel (heel turn).   Q.
3. Step to the side with the R.F. opening into P.P.   Q.
4. Step through with the L.F. in P.P.   S.
   Then go straight into 2, 3, 4, of the Feather Step, or turn on 4 into 2, 3, 4, 5, 6, of Natural Turn.

Rise and fall. Rise at the end of 2 and lower at the end of 3.
Contrary body movement. Used on 1 and 4.
Body sway. Sway slightly to the R. on 2 and 3.

Alternative Ending to the Open Telemark

Wing finish into Reverse Wave

GENTLEMAN

Repeat 1, 2, 3, of the Open Telemark, S.Q.Q., then:—

4.   Cross R.F. over L.F. (feet slightly apart) in P.P.   S.
5, 6.   Hesitate on R.F. whilst partner takes 2 short
        steps round you.   Q.Q.
7.   Step forward with the L.F. outside partner on L.
     side, making this the 1st step of the Reverse   S.
     Wave.

LADY

Repeat 1, 2, 3, 4, of the Open Telemark, S.Q.Q.S., then:—

5.   Short step forward with R.F. (going round partner)   Q.
6.   Short step forward with L.F. (going round partner)   Q.
7.   Step back on to the R.F. (your partner steps out-
     side on L. side) making this the 1st step of the
     Reverse Wave.   S.

How to Construct the Slow Foxtrot

After the Feather Step do one of the following:
1. A three-step forward, R.L.R., turning on the last R. into the Natural Turn.
2. Turn on the last step of the Feather Step into the Reverse Turn, Reverse Wave, or Telemark.
3. Change of Direction.

After the Natural Turn go straight into the Feather Step.
After the Reverse Turn do one of the following:—
1. A three-step forward, R.L.R., turning on the last R. into the Natural Turn.
2. Turn on the last step of the Reverse Turn into the Reverse Wave.
3. Change of Direction.

After the Reverse Wave go straight into the Feather Step.
After the Change of Direction do one of the following:—
1. A Feather Step.
2. Turn on the last step of the Change of Direction into the Reverse Turn or Reverse Wave.

After the above has been mastered, the dancer should have no difficulty in introducing the more advanced figures such as the Telemark and Impetus Turn.

As far as possible try to use right-handed and left-handed turns alternately: doing this will make the dance much more effective.

According to a dancer's ability and experience, so he can add other figures but it is much better to make sure of these standardized figures and amalgamating them before attempting anything more advanced.

THE WALTZ

THE modern Waltz began to evolve about fourteen years ago and it serves as a splendid example to contradict those people who say that modern dancing is always changing. Apart from the fact that the turns are taken on what is known as diagonal lines, the fundamental figures remain the same now as they were then.

The fundamental figures of this dance are simple. There are but three, the Natural Turn, the Reverse Turn and the Changes, i.e., changing from the Natural Turn to the Reverse Turn and vice-versa.

In these three main figures you only use one rhythm to dance to, taking a step to every beat of the music. If one listens to a waltz being played, it is quite easy to distinguish the beats, which recur regularly and consistently throughout the dance: 1, 2, 3, 1, 2, 3, 1, 2, 3, etc. It will be noticed that the 1 is always accentuated.

In the Turns and the Forward changes it is essential that the feet are closed together on the third beat of the music.

Another important feature which it is necessary to observe in order to obtain the correct rhythm, swing and lilt, is the rise. Rise at the end of the first step, continue rising on the second step, coming up on the toes on the third step. Drop again as you take the first step. This rise must be inserted throughout the dance.

The first step of every three must be long, to coincide with the accented beat (1st) in the music.

The Turns and Changes are taken on diagonal lines. This means to say that instead of beginning the figures facing the line of dance they are commenced either diagonally to the wall, as is the case with the Natural Turn, or diagonally to the middle of the room, as is the case with the Reverse Turn. On each turn only three-quarters of a turn is made instead of a full turn. This makes the turns much easier to perform.

The Natural Turn

Begin this figure facing diagonally to the wall, and finish it facing diagonally to middle of room.

GENTLEMAN

1. Step forward with the R.F. turning on it to the R.
2. Step to the side with the L.F. still turning.
3. Close the R.F. up to the L.F.
4. Step back with the L.F. turning on it to the R.
5. Step to the side with the R.F. still turning.
6. Close the L.F. up to the R.F.

Rise and fall. Rise at the end of 1 and lower at the end of 3. Rise again at the end of 4 and lower at the end of 6.

Contrary body movement. Used on 1 and 4.

Body sway. Sway slightly to the R. on 2 and 3, and slightly to the L. on 5 and 6.

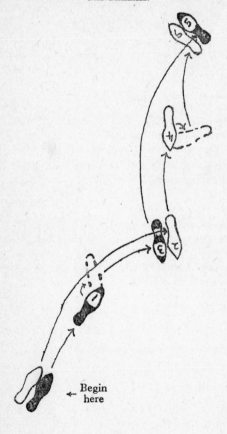

THE NATURAL TURN

GENTLEMAN

Begin
here

The Natural Turn

LADY

1. Step back with the L.F. turning on it to the R.
2. Step to the side with the R.F. still turning.
3. Close the L.F. up to the R.F.
4. Step forward with the R.F. turning on it to the R.
5. Step to the side with the L.F. still turning.
6. Close the R.F. up to the L.F.

Rise and fall. Rise at the end of 1 and lower at the end of 3. Rise again at the end of 4 and lower at the end of 6.

Contrary body movement. Used on 1 and 4.

Body sway. Sway slightly to the L. on 2 and 3, and slightly to the R. on 5 and 6.

THE NATURAL TURN

LADY

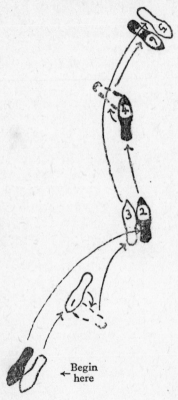

Begin → here

The Reverse Turn

Begin this figure facing diagonally to the middle of room, and finish it facing diagonally to the wall.

GENTLEMAN

1. Step forward with the L.F. turning on it to the L.
2. Step to the side with the R.F. still turning.
3. Close the L.F. up to the R.F.
4. Step back with the R.F. turning on it to the L.
5. Step to the side with the L.F. still turning.
6. Close the R.F. up to the L.F.

Rise and fall. Rise at the end of 1 and lower at the end of 3. Rise again at the end of 4 and lower at the end of 6.

Contrary body movement. Used on 1 and 4.

Body sway. Sway slightly to the L. on 2 and 3, and slightly to the R. on 5 and 6.

The Reverse Turn

GENTLEMAN

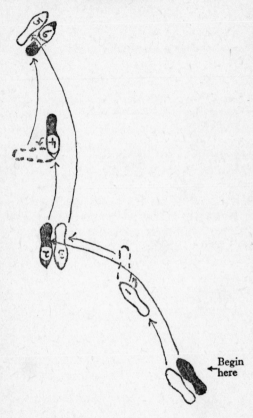

Begin
here

THE REVERSE TURN

LADY

1. Step back with the R.F. turning on it to the L.
2. Step to the side with the L.F. still turning.
3. Close the R.F. up to the L.F.
4. Step forward with the L.F. turning on it to the L.
5. Step to the side with the R.F. still turning.
6. Close the L.F. up to the R.F.

Rise and fall. Rise at the end of 1 and lower at the end of 3. Rise again at the end of 4 and lower at the end of 6.

Contrary body movement. Used on 1 and 4.

Body sway. Sway slightly to the R. on 2 and 3, and slightly to the L. on 5 and 6.

The Reverse Turn

LADY

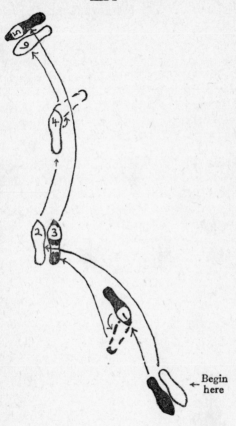

Begin
here

The Forward Change

After a Natural Turn.

GENTLEMAN

1. Step forward with the R.F.
2. Step to the side with the L.F.
3. Close the R.F. up to the L.F.

Rise and fall. Rise at the end of 1 and lower at the end of 3.

Contrary body movement. Used slightly on 1.

Body sway. Sway slightly to the R. on 2 and 3.

LADY

1. Step back with the L.F.
2. Step to the side with the R.F.
3. Close the L.F. up to the R.F.

Rise and fall. Rise at the end of 1 and lower at the end of 3.

Contrary body movement. Used slightly on 1.

Body sway. Sway slightly to the L. on 2 and 3.

NOTE.—After this Forward Change go into the Reverse Turn.

The Forward Change

After a Natural Turn

GENTLEMAN

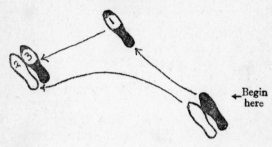

LADY

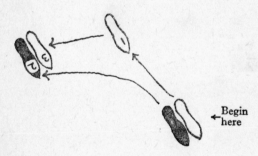

The Forward Change

After a Reverse Turn

GENTLEMAN

1. Step forward with the L.F.
2. Step to the side with the R.F.
3. Close the L.F. up to the R.F.

Rise and fall. Rise at the end of 1 and lower at the end of 3.

Contrary body movement. Used slightly on 1.

Body sway. Sway slightly to the L. on 2 and 3.

LADY

1. Step back with the R.F.
2. Step to the side with the L.F.
3. Close the R.F. up to the L.F.

Rise and fall. Rise at the end of 1 and lower at the end of 3.

Contrary body movement. Used slightly on 1.

Body sway. Sway slightly to the R. on 2 and 3.

Note.—After this Forward Change go into the Natural Turn.

The Forward Change

After a Reverse Turn

GENTLEMAN

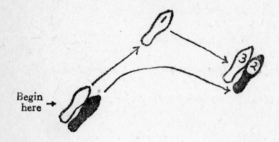

Begin here →

LADY

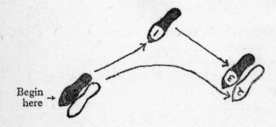

Begin here →

The Backward Change

After 1, 2, 3, of the Natural Turn.

GENTLEMAN

Make only a quarter turn on 1, 2, 3, of the Natural Turn, so that you will begin the Backward Change with your back diagonally to the centre of the room.

1. Step back with the L.F. turning your body slightly (C.B.M.).
2. Step back with the R.F.
3. Step back with the L.F. allowing it to just pass the R.F. and go straight into 4, 5, 6 of the Reverse Turn.

Rise and fall. Rise at the end of 1 and lower at the end of 3.

Contrary body movement. Used on 1.

Body sway. Sway slightly to the L. on 2 and 3.

LADY

1. Step forward with the R.F. turning your body slightly (C.B.M.).
2. Step forward with the L.F.
3. Step forward with the R.F. allowing it to just pass the L.F. and go straight into 4, 5, 6 of the Reverse Turn.

Rise and fall. Rise at the end of 1 and lower at the end of 3.

Contrary body movement. Used on 1.

Body sway. Sway slightly to the R. on 2 and 3.

THE BACKWARD CHANGE

After 1, 2, 3, of the Reverse Turn.

GENTLEMAN
Make only a quarter turn on 1, 2, 3, of the Reverse Turn,
so that you will begin the Backward Change with your
back diagonally to the outside of room—the wall.

1. Step back with the R.F. turning your body slightly
    (C.B.M.).
2. Step back with the L.F.
3. Step back with the R.F. allowing it to just pass the
    L.F. and go straight into 4, 5, 6 of the Natural Turn.

Rise and fall. Rise at the end of 1 and lower at the end
of 3.

Contrary body movement. Used on 1.

Body sway. Sway slightly to the R. on 2 and 3.

LADY
1. Step forward with the L.F. turning your body slightly
    (C.B.M.).
2. Step forward with the R.F.
3. Step forward with the L.F. allowing it to just pass the
    R. F. and go straight into 4, 5, 6, of the Natural Turn.

Rise and fall. Rise at the end of 1 and lower at the end
of 3.

Contrary body movement. Used on 1.

Body sway. Sway slightly to the L. on 2 and 3.

The Natural Spin Turn

GENTLEMAN

1, 2, 3. Do 1, 2, 3 of the Natural Turn, then:—

4.   Step back with the L.F. pivoting on it to the R.

5.   Spin round on the R.F. (keeping it in front of you).

6.   Small step to the side with the L.F.

7, 8, 9.   Step back with the R.F. turning on it to L. and go straight into 5, 6, of the Reverse Turn.

Rise and fall. At the beginning, as in Natural Turn. On the Spin, rise at the end of 5 and lower at the end of 6. At the finish, as in finish of Reverse Turn.

Contrary body movement. Used on 1, 4, 5, 7.

Body sway. At the beginning, sway as in Natural Turn. On the Spin there is no sway. At the finish, sway as in finish of Reverse Turn.

LADY

1, 2, 3. Do 1, 2, 3 of the Natural Turn, then:—

4.   Step forward with the R.F. pivoting on it to the R.

5.   Step back on to the L.F. still turning.

6.   Brush R.F. to L.F. and take short step to side with it.

7, 8, 9.   Step forward with the L.F. turning on it to L. and go straight into 5, 6, of the Reverse Turn.

Rise and fall. At the beginning, as in Natural Turn. On the Spin, rise at the end of 5 and lower at the end of 6. At the finish, as in finish of Reverse Turn.

Contrary body movement. Used on 1, 4, 7. (The lady loses her C.B.M. on 5.)

Body sway. At the beginning, as in Natural Turn. On the Spin there is no sway. At the finish, as in finish of Reverse Turn.

The Reverse Corté

GENTLEMAN

1, 2, 3. Do 1, 2, 3 of the Reverse Turn, then:—

4. Step back with the R.F. turning to the L.

5, 6. Close the L.F. back to the R.F. and hesitate, making a little over a quarter turn to the L.

7. Step back with the L.F. leading your partner outside, and go straight into 5, 6 of the Natural Turn without turning.

Rise and fall. At the beginning, as in Reverse Turn. On the Corté rise at the end of 4 and lower at the end of 6. At the finish as in finish of Natural Turn.

Contrary body movement. Used on 1, 4, 7.

Body sway. At the beginning, as in Reverse Turn. On the Corté, sway slightly to the R. on 5 and 6. At the finish as in finish of Natural Turn.

LADY

1, 2, 3. Do 1, 2, 3 of the Reverse Turn, then:—

4. Step forward with the L.F. turning to the L.

5. Step to the side with the R.F.

6. Close the L.F. up to the R.F.

7. Step forward with the R.F. outside your partner, and go straight into 5, 6 of the Natural Turn without turning.

Rise and fall. At the beginning, as in Reverse Turn. On the Corté, rise at the end of 4 and lower at the end of 6. At the finish, as in finish of Natural Turn.

Contrary body movement. Used on 1, 4, 7.

Body sway. At the beginning, as in Reverse Turn. On the Corté, sway slightly to the L. on 5 and 6. At the finish, as in finish of Natural Turn.

6

The Hesitation Change

This figure is very useful in small or rather crowded ballrooms, as you can quickly get from your Natural into your Reverse Turn, without taking up the space that is required when the Forward or Backward Changes are used in between the turns.

GENTLEMAN

1, 2, 3, 4. Do 1, 2, 3, 4 of the Natural Turn, then:—
5. Pull the R.F. back to the L.F. turning from the L. heel on to the R. heel (feet slightly apart).
6. Hesitate as you brush the L.F. through (close to the R.F.).
7. Step forward with the L.F. going into the Reverse Turn.

Rise and fall. At the beginning, as in Natural Turn. On the Hesitation Change there is no rise.

Contrary body movement. Used on 1, 4, 7.

Body sway. At the beginning, as in Natural Turn. Sway slightly to the L. on 5, 6.

LADY

1, 2, 3, 4. Do 1, 2, 3, 4 of the Natural Turn, then:—
5. Step to the side with the L.F.
6. Brush the R.F. through (close to the L.F.).
7. Step back with the R.F. going into the Reverse Turn.

Rise and fall. At the beginning, as in Natural Turn. On the Hesitation Change there is no rise.

Contrary body movement. Used on 1, 4, 7.

Body sway. At the beginning, as in Natural Turn. Sway slightly to the R. on 5, 6.

THE DOUBLE REVERSE SPIN

Although called the *Double* Reverse Spin, this does not signify that it must be used twice. More often than not, it is only used once at a time.

Whilst the gentleman does 3 steps to 3 beats, the lady does 4 steps to 3 beats, that is why it is counted 1, 2, "and" 3.

GENTLEMAN

1. Step forward with L.F. turning on it to the L.
2. Step to the side with R.F. still turning
   "and"
3. Close L.F. to R.F. completing turn on ball of R.F.—then step forward with L.F. going into the Forward Change L.F., R.F., L.F.

Rise and fall. Rise at the end of 2 and lower at the end of 3.

Contrary body movement. Used on 1.

Body sway. Nil.

LADY

1. Step back with R.F. turning on it to the L.
2. Close L.F. to R.F. turning from R. heel on to L. heel (heel turn)
   "and" Step to side with R.F. still turning.
3. Cross L.F. up in front of R.F. completing turn—then step back with R.F. going into the Forward Change.

Rise and fall. Rise at the end of 2 and lower at the end of 3.

Contrary body movement. Used on 1.

Body sway. Nil.

THE OUTSIDE SPIN

There are one or two different ways of going into an Outside Spin, but the most usual is after No. 6 of the Reverse Corté. Do 1 to 6 of the Reverse Corté then:—

GENTLEMAN

1. Very short step back with L.F. keeping weight on R.F. turning to R. leading partner outside.
2. Spin round on R.F. (keeping it in front of you).
3. Step to the side with L.F. still turning.
   Then step forward with the R.F. into the Natural Turn.

NOTE.—Make one complete turn in this figure.
Rise and fall. Rise at the end of 2 and lower at the end of 3.
Contrary body movement. Used on 1 and 2.
Body sway. Nil.

LADY

1. Step forward with the R.F. outside partner turning to the R.
2. Close the L.F. up to the R.F. still turning.
3. Step forward with the R.F. in front of partner still turning.
   Then step back with the L.F. into the Natural Turn.

NOTE.—Make one complete turn in this figure.
Rise and fall. Rise at the end of 2 and lower at the end of 3.
Contrary body movement. Used on 1 and 3.
Body sway. Nil.

THE OPEN TELEMARK

After the Open Telemark there are one or two different ways of finishing it. They are described below.

GENTLEMAN

1. Step forward with the L.F. turning on it to the L.
2. Step to the side with the R.F. still turning.
3. Step to the side with the L.F. opening into P.P. (facing wall).

Rise and fall. Rise at the end of 2 and lower at the end of 3.

Contrary body movement. Used on 1.

Body sway. Sway slightly to the L. on 2 and 3.

LADY

1. Step back with the R.F. turning on it to the L.
2. Close the L.F. back to the R.F. turning from R. heel on to L. heel (heel turn).
3. Step to the side with the R.F. opening into P.P.

Rise and fall. Rise at the end of 2 and lower at the end of 3.

Contrary body movement. Used on 1.

Body sway. Sway slightly to the R. on 2 and 3.

ALTERNATIVE ENDINGS TO THE OPEN TELEMARK
1.

GENTLEMAN

Repeat 1, 2, 3, of the Open Telemark, then:—

4. Step through with the R.F. in P.P. (facing wall diagonally).
5, 6. Hesitate with weight on R.F. without turning.
 Then step back with the L.F. leading partner outside and go into 5, 6, of the Natural Turn without turning (finish facing diagonally to wall).

LADY

Repeat 1, 2, 3, of the Open Telemark, then:—

4. Step through with the L.F. in P.P. turning to L. (to face partner).
5. Step to the side with the R.F.
6. Close the L.F. up to the R.F.
 Then step forward with the R.F. outside partner and go into 5, 6, of the Natural Turn without turning.

2.

GENTLEMAN

Repeat 1, 2, 3, of the Open Telemark, then:—

4.   Cross R.F. over L.F. (feet slightly apart) in P.P. turning
     on it to the L.
5, 6.   Hesitate on R.F. turning to face middle of room.
     Then step back with the L.F. leading partner outside
     and go into 5, 6, of the Natural Turn.

LADY

Repeat 1, 2, 3, of the Open Telemark, then:—

4.   Step through with the L.F. in P.P.
5.   Step to the side with the R.F. still turning.
6.   Close the L.F. up to the R.F. (facing wall).
     Then step forward with the R.F. outside partner and
     go into 5, 6, of the Natural Turn.

3. (*Wing finish*)

GENTLEMAN

Repeat 1, 2, 3, of the Open Telemark, then:—

4.   Cross R.F. over L.F. (feet slightly apart) in P.P.
5, 6.   Hesitate on R.F. whilst partner takes 2 short steps
     round you.
     Then step forward with the L.F. outside partner on
     L. side, making this the 1st step of a Forward Change,
     Reverse Turn or Double Reverse Spin.

LADY

Repeat 1, 2, 3, of the Open Telemark, then:—

4.   Step through with the L.F. in P.P.
5.   Short step forward with R.F. (going round partner).
6.   Short step forward with L.F. (going round partner).
     Then step back on to the R.F. (your partner steps
     outside on L. side) making this the 1st step of a For-
     ward Change, Reverse Turn or Double Reverse Spin.

How to Construct the Waltz

First of all get thoroughly used to doing a Natural Turn, Forward Change, Reverse Turn, Forward Change. When you can do this sequence keeping the correct alignment you will have little difficulty in working the other figures in. Occasionally use the Backward Changes. Going round corners you will find it quite comfortable to repeat two or three (according to shape of room) Natural Turns following one another. Never use more than one Reverse Turn at a time unless you are a thoroughly experienced dancer and understand the correct alignment in which to take it. Do not try to use a Reverse Turn on a corner.

After the above has been mastered, the dancer should have no difficulty in introducing the more advanced figures such as the Natural Spin Turn, the Reverse Corté, the Hesitation Change and the Double Reverse Spin.

According to a dancer's ability and experience, so he can add other figures, but it is much better to make sure of these standardized figures and amalgamating them before attempting anything more advanced.

A REMINDER

Do not forget that the diagrams showing the positions of the feet in the different dances are not intended to be mathematically exact, but merely to show the pattern made in the various figures.

For full details of the abbreviations and explanations see pages 35 and 36.

THE QUICKSTEP

THIS dance is undoubtedly the most popular dance in the world to-day.

For those who cannot give the time, or are not keen enough to learn the four standard dances, the Quickstep is the one that they should know more than any other.

There are two fundamental steps in this dance, the Walk and the Chassé. Every standardized figure is made up of these two steps.

THE WALK FORWARD

This is the same as in the Slow Foxtrot, only it is quicker. Take a gliding step straight from the hips, skimming your foot lightly along the floor. When you are out to your full stretch you should be on the heel of your front foot: immediately lower on to the flat foot. Your back foot should now be on the toes before it is released to move forward. Repeat with the opposite leg. Each walk takes two beats of the music and is counted "slow". (For details of the carriage of weight in the Walk, see the chapter on Balance.) Keep moving forward continuously the whole time and do not release your back foot until the last possible moment.

The Walk Backward

This is the same as in the Slow Foxtrot, only it is quicker. Swing your leg well back from the hip, going on to the toes first and keeping your weight on your front foot. As you continue, your weight should be carried between your feet, and the toes of the front foot should leave the floor so that the pressure is on the front heel. Your weight is then transferred on to the ball of the back foot, but your weight is still forward, as your back heel is off the floor. Continue and do not lower your back heel until the other foot passes it. Repeat with the opposite leg. Each walk takes two beats of the music and is counted "slow". (For fuller details, see the chapter on Balance.) With your weight forward, keep moving backward continuously the whole time and do not release your front foot hurriedly: pull it back with pressure on the heel.

The Chassés

These may be taken in different ways but it is always, a step with one foot, close the other foot up to it, then move the original foot again. A chassé is counted quick, quick, slow, and takes four beats of the music. In the different figures where they are used, they are clearly described.

The Natural Turn

This figure is not used very much now. It is kept in the Quickstep because other figures are built up out of it. The Natural Pivot Turn is the figure that is used in place of it.

GENTLEMAN

1.	Step forward with the R.F. turning on it to the R.	S.
2.	Step to the side with the L.F. still turning.	Q.
3.	Close the R.F. up to the L.F.	Q.
4.	Step back with the L.F. turning on it to the R.	S.
5.	Pull the R.F. back to the L.F. (feet slightly apart) turning from the L. heel on to the R. heel.	S.
6.	Step forward with the L.F.	S.

Chassé { 2, 3, 4 }

Rise and fall. Rise at the end of 1 and lower at the end of 3.

Contrary body movement. Used on 1, 4, 6.

Body sway. Sway slightly to the R. on 2 and 3.

When used, only three-quarters of a turn should be made on the complete figure.

The Natural Turn

GENTLEMAN

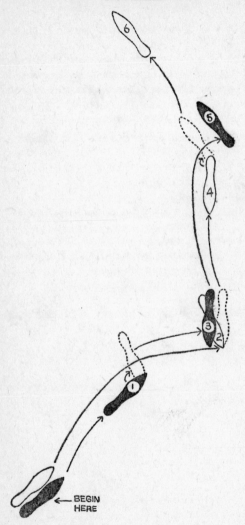

BEGIN
HERE

The Natural Turn

This figure is not used very much now. It is kept in the Quickstep because other figures are built up out of it. The Natural Pivot Turn is the figure that is used in place of it.

LADY

1.   Step back with the L.F. turning on it to the R.   S.

Chassé {
2.   Step to the side with the R.F. still turning.   Q.
3.   Close the L.F. up to the R.F.   Q.
4.   Step forward with the R.F. turning on it to the R.   S.

5.   Step to the side with the L.F.   S.
6.   Brush the R.F. through (close to the L.F.) and step back with it.   S.

Rise and fall. Rise at the end of 1 and lower at the end of 3.

Contrary body movement. Used on 1, 4, 6.

Body sway. Sway slightly to the L. on 2 and 3.

The Natural Turn

LADY

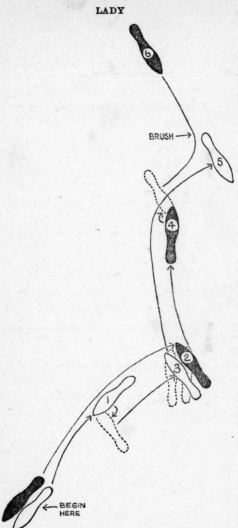

The Natural Pivot Turn

GENTLEMAN

This is the best and most popular right-handed turn used in the Quickstep.

	1.	Step forward with the R.F. turning on it to the R.	S.
Chassé	2.	Step to the side with the L.F. still turning.	Q.
	3.	Close the R.F. up to the L.F.	Q.
	4.	Step back with the L.F. pivoting about a half turn to the R. (keeping R.F. in front of you).	S.
	5.	Step forward on to R.F. still turning.	S.

NOTE.—The Natural Pivot Turn is nearly always followed by the Quarter Turns, so No. 5 described above would be No. 1 of the Quarter Turns.

Make approximately one complete turn on this figure.

Rise and fall. Rise at the end of 1 and lower at the end of 3.

Contrary body movement. Used on 1, 4, 5.

Body sway. Sway slightly to the R. on 2 and 3.

The Natural Pivot Turn

GENTLEMAN

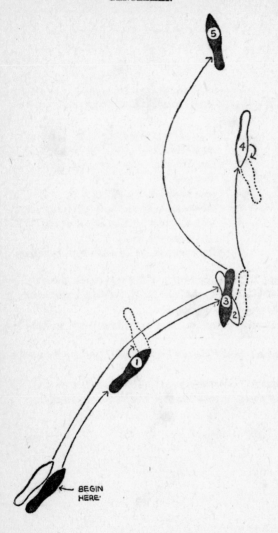

BEGIN HERE

The Natural Pivot Turn

LADY

This is the best and most popular right-handed turn used in the Quickstep.

	1.	Step back with the L.F. turning on it to the R.	S
Chassé	2.	Step to the side with the R.F. still turning.	Q.
	3.	Close the L.F. up to the R.F.	Q.
	4.	Step forward with the R.F. pivoting on it to the R.	S.
	5.	Step back on to the L.F. still turning.	S.

Note.—The Natural Pivot Turn is nearly always followed by the Quarter Turns, so No. 5 described above would be No. 1 of the Quarter Turns.

Make approximately one complete turn on this figure.

Rise and fall. Rise at the end of 1 and lower at the end of 3.

Contrary body movement. Used on 1, 4 and 5.

Body sway. Sway slightly to the L. on 2 and 3.

The Natural Pivot Turn

LADY

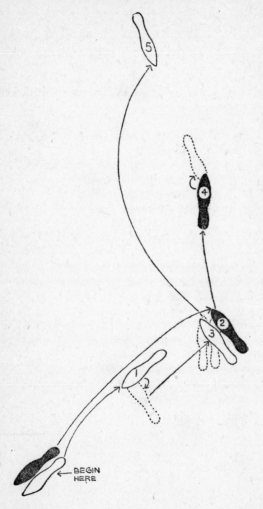

The Reverse Turn

This figure is not used in full, only in parts. It is kept in the Quickstep because other figures are built up out of it. The Chassé Reverse Turn is the figure that is used in place of it.

GENTLEMAN

1.	Step forward with the L.F. turning on it to the L.	S.
2.	Step to the side with the R.F. still turning.	S.
3.	Step back with the L.F.	S.
4.	Step back with the R.F. turning on it to the L.	S.
5. }	Close the L.F. back to the R.F. turning to the L.	
6. }	on the R. heel (heel pivot).	Q.Q.
7.	Step forward with the L.F.	S.

On 5, 6, the gentleman is making only one step, doing what is known as a heel pivot. This heel pivot is substituted for a chassé which would look unfinished. Whilst he is making this one step, the lady is making two steps, that is why it is counted Q.Q.

Rise and fall. Rise at the end of 2 and lower at the end of 3. There is also a slight "body rise" on 5, 6. This is obtained by bracing the R. knee.

Contrary body movement. Used on 1, 4, 7.

Body sway. Sway slightly to the L. on 2 and 3, and slightly to the R. on 5 and 6.

The Reverse Turn

GENTLEMAN

Begin
← here

THE REVERSE TURN

This figure is not used in full, only in parts. It is kept in the Quickstep because other figures are built up out of it. The Chassé Reverse Turn is the figure that is used in place of it.

LADY

1. Step back with the R.F. turning on it to the L. S.
2. Close the L.F. back to the R.F. turning from the R. heel on to the L. heel (heel turn). S.
3. Step forward with the R.F. S.
4. Step forward with the L.F. turning on it to the L. S.

Chassé
{
5. Step to the side with the R.F. Q.
6. Close the L.F. up to the R.F. Q.
7. Step back with the R.F. S.
}

Rise and fall. Rise at the end of 2 and lower at the end of 3. Rise again slightly at the end of 5 and lower at the end of 6.

Contrary body movement. Used on 1, 4, 7.

Body sway. Sway slightly to the R. on 2 and 3, and slightly to the L. on 5 and 6.

THE REVERSE TURN
LADY

The Chassé Reverse Turn

This is the most popular left-handed turn used in the Quickstep.

GENTLEMAN

	1.	Step forward with the L.F. turning on it to the L.	S.
Chassé {	2.	Step to the side with the R.F. still turning.	Q.
	3.	Close the L.F. up to the R.F.	Q.
	4.	Step back with the R.F. turning on it to the L.	S.
	5. }	Close the L.F. back to the R.F. turning	
	6. }	to L. on R. heel (heel pivot).	Q.Q.
	7.	Step forward with the L.F.	S.

On 5, 6, the gentleman is making only one step, doing what is known as a heel pivot. This heel pivot is substituted for a chassé which would look unfinished. Whilst he is making this one step, the lady is making two steps, that is why it is counted Q.Q.

Rise and fall. Rise at the end of 1 and lower at the end of 3. There is also a slight "body rise" on 5, 6. This is obtained by bracing the R. knee.

Contrary body movement. Used on 1, 4, 7.

Body sway. Sway slightly to the L. on 2 and 3, and slightly to the R. on 5 and 6.

The Chassé Reverse Turn

GENTLEMAN

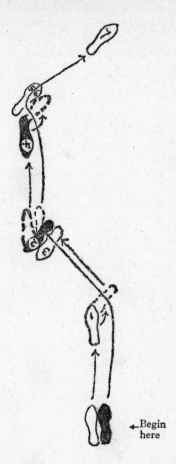

←Begin here

The Chassé Reverse Turn

This is the most popular left-handed turn used in the Quickstep.

LADY

	1.	Step back with the R.F. turning on it to the L.	S.
Chassé	2.	Short step to side with the L.F. still turning.	Q.
	3.	Close the R.F. up to the L.F.	Q.
	4.	Step forward with the L.F. turning on it to the L.	S.
Chassé	5.	Step to the side with the R.F. still turning.	Q.
	6.	Close the L.F. up to the R.F.	Q.
	7.	Step back with the R.F.	S.

Rise and fall. Rise at the end of 1 and lower at the end of 3. Rise again slightly at the end of 5 and lower at the end of 6.

Contrary body movement. Used on 1, 4, 7.

Body sway. Sway slightly to the R. on 2 and 3, and slightly to the L. on 5 and 6.

The Chassé Reverse Turn

LADY

← Begin
here

The Quarter Turns

This is the most important and popular figure in the Quickstep. It is called the Quarter Turns because a quarter turn to the R. is made on the first part, and a quarter turn to the L. on the last part. The first part is the same as the first part of the Natural Turn, and the last part is the same as the last part of the Reverse Turn. In other words you do the first part of the Natural Turn followed immediately by the last part of the Reverse Turn.

GENTLEMAN

Begin this figure facing diagonally to the wall.

1.	Step forward with the R.F. turning on it to the R.	S.
2.	Step to the side with the L.F. still turning.	Q.
3.	Close the R.F. up to the L.F.	Q.
4.	Step diagonally back with the L.F.	S.
5.	Step back with the R.F. turning on it to the L.	S.
6. }	Close the L.F. back to the R.F. turning	
7. }	to the L. on the R. heel (heel pivot)	Q.Q.
8.	Step forward with the L.F.	S.

Chassé { 2, 3, 4

Make a quarter turn to the R. on 1, 2, 3, 4, and a quarter turn to the L. on 5, 6, 7, 8. If following with any reverse figure, turn more on 6, 7, 8 (heel pivot) to finish facing L.O.D.

Rise and all. Rise at the end of 1 and lower at the end of 4. There is also a slight "body rise" on 6, 7. This is obtained by bracing the R. knee.

Contrary body movement. Used on 1, 5, 8.

Body sway. Sway slightly to the R. on 2 and 3, and slightly to the R. on 6 and 7.

The Quarter Turns

GENTLEMAN

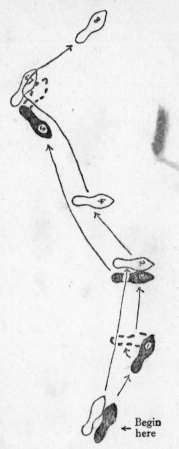

Begin
here

THE QUARTER TURNS

This is the most important and popular figure in the Quickstep. It is called the Quarter Turns because a quarter turn to the R. is made on the first part, and a quarter turn to the L. on the last part. The first part is the same as the first part of the Natural Turn, and the last part is the same as the last part of the Reverse Turn. In other words you do the first part of the Natural Turn followed immediately by the last part of the Reverse Turn.

LADY

	1.	Step back with the L.F. turning on it to the R.	S.
Chassé	2.	Step to the side with the R.F. still turning.	Q.
	3.	Close the L.F. up to the R.F.	Q.
	4.	Step diagonally forward with the R.F.	S.
	5.	Step forward with the L.F. turning on it to the L.	S.
Chassé	6.	Step to the side with the R.F.	Q.
	7.	Close the L.F. up to the R.F.	Q.
	8.	Step back with the R.F.	S.

Make a quarter turn to the R. on 1, 2, 3, 4, and a quarter turn to the L. on 5, 6, 7, 8.

Rise and fall. Rise at the end of 1 and lower at the end of 4. Rise again slightly at the end of 6 and lower at the end of 7.

Contrary body movement. Used on 1, 5, 8.

Body sway. Sway slightly to the L. on 2 and 3, and slightly to the L. on 6 and 7.

THE QUARTER TURNS

LADY

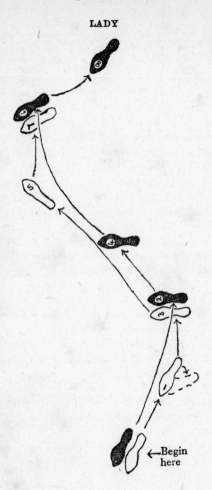

←Begin here

THE ZIG-ZAG

This figure is called the Zig-Zag because the pattern of it is zig-zag.

GENTLEMAN

1. Step forward with the L.F. turning on it to the L.   S.
2. Step to the side with the R.F. still turning.   S.
3. Step back (and across behind R.F.) with L.F. leading partner outside.   S.
4. Close the R.F. back to the L.F. turning from the L. heel on to the R. heel (feet slightly apart).   S.
5. Step forward with the L.F.   S.

Make just over a quarter turn to the L. on 1, 2, and approximately a quarter turn (more or less) to the R. on 3, 4, 5.

NOTE.—If used near the end of the room the Zig-Zag should be finished facing diagonally to the middle of room as shown in the diagram. If used anywhere else it should be finished facing the L.O.D. which means that more turn would have to be made on 3, 4.

Rise and fall. Nil.
Contrary body movement. Used on 1, 3, 5.
Body sway. Nil.

THE ZIG-ZAG

GENTLEMAN

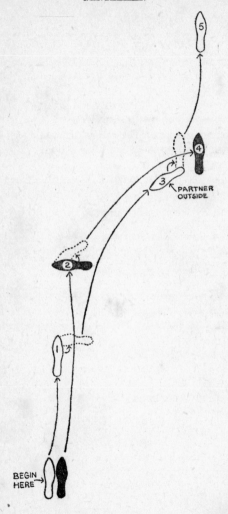

The Zig-Zag

This figure is called the Zig-Zag because the pattern of it is zig-zag.

LADY

1. Step back with the R.F. turning on it to the L.   S.
2. Close the L.F. back to the R.F. turning from the R. heel on to the L. heel (heel turn).   S.
3. Step forward with the R.F. outside your partner.   S.
4. Step to the side with the L.F.   S.
5. Brush the R.F. through (close to the L.F.) and step back with it.   S.

Make just over a quarter turn to the L. on 1, 2 and a quarter turn to the R. on 3, 4, 5.

Rise and fall. Nil.
Contrary body movement. Used on 1, 3, 5.
Body sway. Nil.

THE ZIG-ZAG

LADY

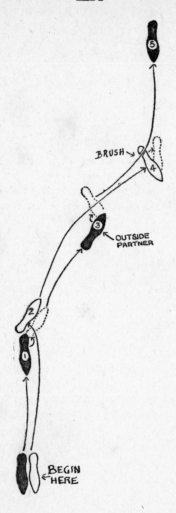

BRUSH

OUTSIDE
PARTNER

BEGIN
HERE

8

THE CROSS CHASSÉ

GENTLEMAN

	1.	Step forward with the L.F.	S.
Chassé	2.	Very short step to the side with the R.F.	Q.
	3.	Close the L.F. up to the R.F.	Q.
	4.	Step forward with the R.F. outside your partner.	S.

Rise and fall. Rise at the end of 1 and lower at the end of 3.

Contrary body movement. Used on 1 and 4.

Body sway. Sway slightly to the L. on 2 and 3.

LADY

	1.	Step back with the R.F.	S.
Chassé	2.	Very short step to the side with the L.F.	Q.
	3.	Close the R.F. up to the L.F.	Q.
	4.	Step back with the L.F. (your partner steps outside you).	S.

Rise and fall. Rise at the end of 1 and lower at the end of 3.

Contrary body movement. Used on 1 and 4.

Body sway. Sway slightly to the R. on 2 and 3.

THE CROSS CHASSÉ

GENTLEMAN

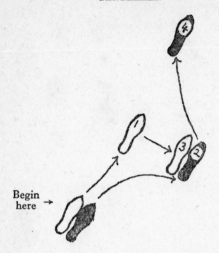

LADY

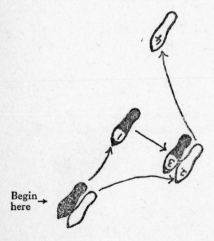

THE DRAG

This figure is not unlike a Cross Chassé. The pattern however is slightly different and also the timing. It is usually used after the 4th step of the Reverse Turn or after the 5th step of the Quarter Turns. In both cases this means to say that the gentleman will be back on his R.F. He then does the Drag as follows:—

GENTLEMAN

1. Step forward on to the L.F. turning slightly to the L.   Q.
2. Step diagonally back on to the R.F.   Q.
3. Drag the L.F. up to the R.F.   S.
4. Step forward with the R.F. outside your partner.   S.

Rise and fall. Rise at the end of 2 and lower at the end of 3.

Contrary body movement. Used on 1 and 4.

Body sway. Sway slightly to the L. on 2 and 3.

The Drag

GENTLEMAN

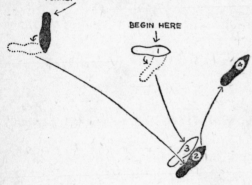

THIS IS FOURTH STEP OF
REVERSE PIVOT TURN, OR
FIFTH STEP OF QUARTER
TURNS.

BEGIN HERE

The Drag

This figure is not unlike a Cross Chassé. The pattern however, is slightly different and also the timing. It is usually used after the 4th step of the Reverse Turn, or after the 5th step of the Quarter Turns. In both cases this means to say that the lady will be forward on her L.F. She then does the Drag as follows:—

LADY

1. Step back on to the R.F. turning slightly to the L.   Q.
2. Step diagonally forward on to the L.F.   Q.
3. Drag the R.F. up to the L.F.   S.
4. Step back with the L.F. (your partner steps outside you).   S.

Rise and fall. Rise at the end of 2 and lower at the end of 3.

Contrary body movement. Used on 1 and 4.

Body sway. Sway slightly to the R. on 2 and 3.

THE DRAG

LADY

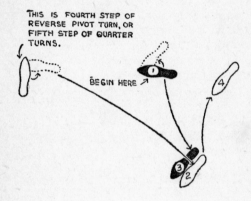

THIS IS FOURTH STEP OF
REVERSE PIVOT TURN, OR
FIFTH STEP OF QUARTER
TURNS.

BEGIN HERE ↗

The Change of Direction

GENTLEMAN

1. Step diagonally forward with the R.F. turning on it to the L.   S.
2. Brush the L.F. up to the R.F. turning on the R.F. to the L. (relaxing the knees well).   S.
3. Step forward with the L.F.   S.

Rise and fall. Nil.
Contrary body movement. Used on 3.
Body sway. Sway slightly to the L. on 1, 2.

LADY

1. Step diagonally back with the L.F. turning on it to the L.   S.
2. Brush the R.F. up to the L.F. turning on the L.F. to the L. (relaxing the knees well).   S.
3. Step back with the R.F.   S.

Rise and fall. Nil.
Contrary body movement. Used on 3.
Body sway. Sway slightly to the R. on 1, 2.

The Double Reverse Spin

GENTLEMAN

Although called the Double Reverse Spin, this does not signify that it must be used twice. It is better to use it only once at a time.

Whilst the gentleman does three steps the lady does four, that is why it is counted slow, slow, quick, quick.

1. Step forward with the L.F. turning on it to the L.   S.
2. Step to the side with the R.F. still turning.   S.
3. 4. Close the L.F. up to the R.F. completing turn on ball of R.F. (toe pivot).   Q.Q.
    After this, step forward with the L.F.

Rise and fall. Rise at the end of 2 and lower at the end of 4.

Contrary body movement. Used on 1.

Body sway. Nil.

LADY

1. Step back with the R.F. turning on it to the L.   S.
2. Close the L.F. back to the R.F. turning from the R. heel on to the L. heel (heel turn).   S.
3. Step to the side with the R.F. still turning.   Q.
4. Cross the L.F. up in front of the R.F. completing turn.   Q.
    After this, step back with the R.F.

Rise and fall. Rise at the end of 2 and lower at the end of 4.

Contrary body movement. Used on 1.

Body sway. Nil.

THE RUNNING ZIG-ZAG

GENTLEMAN

Do 1, 2, of the Zig-Zag S.S. then:—

3. Step back with the L.F. turning on it to the R. partner outside.   Q.
4. Short step to the side with the R.F. still turning slightly.   Q.
5. Step forward with the L.F. preparing to step outside partner.   S.
6. Step forward with the R.F. outside partner.   S.

Rise and fall. Rise at the end of 3 and lower at the end of 5.

Contrary body movement. Used on 1, 3, 6.

Body sway. Sway slightly to the L. on 4 and 5.

LADY

Do 1, 2, of the Zig-Zag S.S. then:—

3. Step forward with the R.F. outside partner turning on it to the R.   Q.
4. Step to the side with the L.F. still turning slightly.   Q.
5. Step back with the R.F.   S.
6. Step back with the L.F. (your partner steps outside you).   S.

Rise and fall. Rise at the end of 3 and lower at the end of 5.

Contrary body movement. Used on 1, 3, 6.

Body sway. Sway slightly to the R. on 4 and 5.

THE NATURAL SPIN TURN

GENTLEMAN

1, 2, 3, 4, 5. Do 1, 2, 3, 4, 5, of the Natural Pivot Turn, S.Q.Q.S.S. then:—

6. Short step to the side with the L.F. still turning slightly.   S.

7. Step back with the R.F. turning on it to the L.   S.
   Then go straight into 6, 7, 8, of the Quarter Turns, or pivot on No. 7 and go straight into the Drag.

Rise and fall. At the beginning, as in Natural Pivot Turn. On the Spin, rise at the end of 5 and lower at the end of 6.

Contrary body movement. Used on 1, 4, 5, 7.

Body sway. At the beginning, as in Natural Pivot Turn. On the Spin there is no sway.

LADY

1, 2, 3, 4, 5. Do 1, 2, 3, 4, 5, of the Natural Pivot Turn, S.Q.Q.S.S. then:—

6. Brush R.F. to L.F. and take short step to side with it.   S.

7. Step forward with the L.F. turning on it to the L.   S.
   Then go straight into 6, 7, 8, of the Quarter Turns, or pivot on No. 7 and go straight into the Drag.

Rise and fall. At the beginning, as in Natural Pivot Turn. On the Spin, rise at the end of 5 and lower at the end of 6.

Contrary body movement. Used on 1, 4, 7. (The lady loses her C.B.M. on 5.)

Body sway. At the beginning, as in Natural Pivot Turn. On the Spin there is no sway.

THE REVERSE PIVOT TURN

Actually there are 4 steps in this figure but a fifth step is described to enable readers to follow what comes after the Reverse Pivot Turn.

GENTLEMAN

Do 1, 2, 3, of the Reverse Turn, S.S.S., then:—
4.   Step back with the R.F. pivoting on it to the L.   S.
5.   Step forward on to the L.F.   S. or Q.

NOTE.—On No. 4, the amount of pivot should vary from one-eighth to half a turn according to which figure you use after it. Also No. 5 will be S. or Q. according to which figure you decide to go into. If the Drag make about a quarter of a turn on 4, and No. 5 will be the first step of the Drag— Q. If the Double Reverse Spin make about a third of a turn on 4, and No. 5 will be the first step of the Double Reverse Spin—S.

Rise and fall. At the beginning, rise and lower as in Reverse Turn. On the pivot there is no rise.

Contrary body movement. Used on 1, 4, 5.

Body sway. At the beginning, sway as in Reverse Turn. On the pivot there is no sway.

LADY

Do 1, 2, 3, of the Reverse Turn, S.S.S., then:—
4.   Step forward with the L.F. pivoting on it to the L.   S.
5.   Step back on to the R.F.   S. or Q.

NOTE.—See notes on gentleman's steps.

Rise and fall. At the beginning, rise and lower as in Reverse Turn. On the pivot there is no rise.

Contrary body movement. Used on 1, 4, 5.

Body sway. At the beginning, sway as in Reverse Turn. On the pivot there is no sway.

THE CORTÉ

Do 1, 2, 3, 4, of the Quarter Turns, then:—

GENTLEMAN

1. Step back with the R.F. turning on it to the L.   S.
2. ⎰ Close the L.F. back to the R.F. turning to the L. on
3. ⎱   the R.F.   Q.Q.
4. Step back with the L.F. leading partner outside.   S.

Rise and fall. Nil.
Contrary body movement. Used on 1, 4.
Body sway. Sway slightly to the R. on 2 and 3.

LADY

1. Step forward with the L.F. turning on it to the L.   S.
2. Step to the side with the R.F.   Q.
3. Close the L.F. up to the R.F.   Q.
4. Step forward with the R.F. outside your partner.   S.

Rise and fall. Nil.
Contrary body movement. Used on 1, 4.
Body sway. Sway slightly to the L. on 2 and 3.

Alternative Endings to the Corté

The gentleman's steps are described, the lady's being the exact opposite unless otherwise mentioned.

Heel Pull Finish

Do 1, 2, 3, 4, of the Corté, S.Q.Q.S., then:—

GENTLEMAN

5. Close the R.F. back to the L.F. turning from the L. heel on to the R. heel (heel turn with feet slightly apart).   S.
6. Step forward with the L.F.   S.

LADY

5. Step to the side with the L.F.   S.
6. Brush the R.F. through (close to the L.F.) and step back with it.   S.

Check Finish

Do 1, 2, 3, 4, of the Corté S.Q.Q.S., checking on No. 4, and immediately stepping forward on to the R.F. still outside partner (S) making this the first step of the Quarter Turns.

Running Finish

Do 1, 2, 3, 4, of the Corté S.Q.Q.S., then:—

5. Short step to side with R.F.   Q.
6. Step forward with the L.F. preparing to step outside partner.   Q.
7. Step forward with the R.F. outside partner.   S.

Rise and fall. Rise at the end of 4 and lower at the end of 6.

Contrary body movement. Used on 1, 4, 7.

Body sway. Sway slightly to the L. on 5 and 6. (The lady sways to the R. on 5 and 6.)

THE CROSS SWIVEL

This figure is usually used after the Quarter Turns. No. 1 described below would therefore be the last step of the Quarter Turns. Face diagonally to the wall to begin this figure.

GENTLEMAN

1. Step forward with the L.F. turning on it slightly to the L.   S.
2. Close the R.F. up to the L.F. keeping weight on L.F.   S.
3. Step forward with the R.F. outside partner.   S.

Rise and fall. Nil.
Contrary body movement. Used on 1 and 3.
Body sway. Sway slightly to the L. on 2.

NOTE.—If used at the end of the room the Cross Swivel can be followed by the Quarter Turns. A better ending which can be used at any time, is to use the Running Finish as given on next page.

LADY

1. Step back with the R.F. turning on it slightly to the L.   S.
2. Close the L.F. up to the R.F. keeping weight on R.F.   S.
3. Step back with the L.F. (your partner steps outside).   S.

Rise and fall. Nil.
Contrary body movement. Used on 1 and 3.
Body sway. Sway slightly to the R. on 2.

Alternative ending to the Cross Swivel. The gentleman's steps are described, the lady's being the exact opposite.

RUNNING FINISH

Do a Cross Swivel, S.S.S., then:—
Balance back on to the L.F. partner still outside
    going straight into 3, 4, 5, 6, of the Running
    Zig-Zag.   Q.Q.S.S.

THE IMPETUS TURN

GENTLEMAN

Do 1, 2, 3, of the Natural Turn, then:—
1. Step back with the L.F. turning on it to the R.   S.
2. Close the R.F. back to the L.F. (heel turn) making
    just over three-quarters of a turn to the R.   S.
3. Short step diagonally back with the L.F.   S.
4. Step back with the R.F. turning on it to the L.
    and go straight into 5, 6, 7, of the Reverse Turn,
    or pivot on No. 4 and go straight into the Drag.   S.

Rise and fall. Rise at the end of 2 and lower at the end of 3.
    Contrary body movement. Used on 1 and 4.
    Body sway. Sway slightly to the L. on 2 and 3.

THE IMPETUS TURN

LADY

Do 1, 2, 3, of the Natural Turn, then:—

1. Step forward with the R.F. turning on it to the R.   S.
2. Short step to the side with L.F. still turning.   S.
3. Brush R.F. up to L.F. and immediately take a short
   step diagonally forward with it.   S.
4. Step forward with the L.F. turning on it to the L.
   and go straight into 5, 6, 7, of the Reverse Turn,
   or pivot on No. 4 and go straight into the Drag.   S.

Rise and fall. Rise at the end of 2 and lower at the end
of 3.

Contrary body movement. Used on 1 and 4.

Body sway. Sway slightly to the L. on 2 and 3.

The Running Right Turn

GENTLEMAN

Do 1, 2, 3, 4, of the Natural Pivot Turn.   S.Q.Q.S.
Followed immediately by 1, 2, 3, of the Natural
      Turn in Slow Foxtrot preparing to lead
      partner outside on 3, counting it   S.S.S.
Followed immediately by 3, 4, 5, 6, of the Run-
      ning Zig-Zag.   Q.Q.S.S.

Rise and fall. Rise at the end of 1 and lower at the end
of 3. Rise again at the end of 6 and lower at the end of 7.
Rise again at the end of 8 and lower at the end of 10.
      Contrary body movement. Used on 1, 4, 5, 8, 11.
      Body sway. Sway slightly to the R. on 2 and 3. Sway
slightly to the R. on 6 and 7. Sway slightly to the L. on 9
and 10.

LADY

Do 1, 2, 3, 4, of the Natural Pivot Turn.   S.Q.Q.S.
Followed immediately by 1, 2, 3, of the Natural
      Turn in Slow Foxtrot, counting it   S.S.S.
Followed immediately by 3, 4, 5, 6, of the Run-
      ning Zig-Zag.   Q.Q.S.S.

Rise and fall. Rise at the end of 1 and lower at the end
of 3. Rise again at the end of 6 and lower at the end of 7.
Rise again at the end of 8 and lower at the end of 10.
      Contrary body movement. Used on 1, 4, 5, 8, 11.
      Body sway. Sway slightly to the L. on 2 and 3. Sway
slightly to the L. on 6 and 7. Sway slightly to the R. on
9 and 10.

The Side Step

This figure is not a recognized basic figure of the Quick-step, but it is given herewith because it is one of the most useful figures for a crowded ballroom.

It is taken sideways to the line of dance, the gentleman facing the wall.

GENTLEMAN

Chassé
1. Step to the side with the L.F.   Q.
2. Half close the R.F. up to the L.F.   Q.
3. Step to the side again with the L.F.   S.
4. Close the R.F. up to the L.F.   S.
Repeat *ad lib.*

Rise and fall. Nil.
Contrary body movement. Nil.
Body sway. Sway very slightly to the L. on 1, to the R. on 2, to the L. on 3, to the R. on 4.

LADY

Chassé
1. Step to the side with the R.F.   Q.
2. Half close the L.F. up to the R.F.   Q.
3. Step to the side again with the R.F.   S.
4. Close the L.F. up to the R.F.   S.
Repeat *ad lib.*

Rise and fall. Nil.
Contrary body movement. Nil.
Body sway. Sway very slightly to the R. on 1, to the L. on 2, to the R. on 3, to the L. on 4.

How to Construct the Quickstep

Try to avoid walking in between each figure. As far as possible amalgamate the different figures by making the last step of one figure, the first step of the next.

Use the Quarter Turns as the basis of the dance. To go into all the reverse figures of the Quickstep do so from the last step of the Quarter Turns. You should make the last step of the Quarter Turns, the first step of whichever reverse figure you decide to use.

Use the Cross Chassé after the Quarter Turns, by making the last step of the Quarter Turns, the first step of the Cross Chassé.

Follow the Cross Chassé or the Drag by the Quarter Turns or the Natural Pivot Turn.

Follow the Natural Pivot Turn by the Quarter Turns.

Follow the Zig-Zag with the Natural Pivot Turn or the Quarter Turns.

As far as possible try to use right-handed and left-handed turns alternately: doing this will make the dance much more effective.

According to a dancer's ability and experience, so he can add other figures, but it is much better to make sure of these standardized figures and amalgamating them before attempting anything more advanced.

A REMINDER

Do not forget that the diagrams showing the positions of the feet in the different dances are not intended to be mathematically exact, but merely to show the pattern made in the various figures.

For full details of the abbreviations and explanations see pages 35 and 36.

THE TANGO

THE Tango is now a firmly established dance. It is exceedingly popular in the numerous dance halls throughout the country and is played frequently in many of the smarter ballrooms.

In its most simple and teachable form, it is the easiest of the four standard dances. I am not suggesting however, that the finished or competition Tango is easier than the other dances, but I will go so far as to say that it is no more difficult.

The " track " of the Tango is to curve forward and backward steps inwards—slightly towards the middle of the floor. This involves what is known as contrary body movement position when stepping forwards with the left foot or back with the right. This should not be attempted until the pupil has a fair knowledge of the dance and can perform the first five basic figures with ease.

The Tango hold differs from the other dances in three respects. One's partner is held slightly more to one side—on the right hip; the man's left forearm is bent inwards a little more, and his right hand is placed farther round his partner. This makes the hold more compact.

Photo by Tunbridge

THE TANGO HOLD

The Tango is unique in other respects. It is the only dance in which the feet are picked up ever so slightly from the floor. You do not glide your steps as you do in the other dances, and for this reason the knees are relaxed more than usual. If you glide your step along the floor you will observe that your knee is kept comparatively straight, but the moment you pick your foot up slightly the knee must bend a little more.

There is no body sway. Your shoulders must be parallel to the floor throughout the dance. Also there must be no twisting or turning from the waist.

There is no rise and fall: Tango must be kept quite flat throughout.

Every "slow" step should be held until the last possible moment before moving the other leg. The correct observance of this rule will do more than almost anything to ensure your Tango looking like a Tango.

When you have made fair progress in this dance, another point to remember is that there is a great deal of finesse in the correct closing of the feet on the majority of "slow" steps such as the 4th step of the Promenade, 4th step of the Back Corté, 6th step of the Basic Reverse Turn. On all these closes, the right foot should be closed up to the left foot with a rather staccato movement, the right toe level with the left instep and turned in slightly so that the right knee can be tucked in to the left one. The lady here does not observe the counterpart, but does exactly the same as the gentleman.

The Walk Forward

Take a natural length step forward, picking the foot up ever so slightly, and when out to the full extent, place it down on to the heel first going immediately on to the flat foot. Keep the back foot behind you until the last possible moment before stepping forward with it. Repeat with the opposite leg. Each walk takes one beat of the music and is counted "slow". (For details of the carriage of weight in the Walk, see the chapter on Balance.)

When you are fairly proficient, endeavour to curve your walking steps inwards—slightly towards the middle of the floor. This will make you step into a contrary body movement position whenever you step forward with the L.F. In other words, lock your thighs when you step forward with the L.F., and unlock them when you step forward with the R.F.

This latter "locking and unlocking" should be applied to every normal step forward in the Tango, where your partner is in front of you: it does not apply in outside or promenade figures.

The Walk Backward

Swing the leg back from the hip. When out to the full extent, the toes should meet the floor first immediately lowering on to the ball of the foot (with the heel off the floor). Your weight should now be evenly balanced between your feet and the toes of your front foot should be off the floor slightly so that the pressure is on the front heel. Your weight is then transferred on to the ball of the back foot. Continue and do not lower the back heel until the other foot passes it. Hold the front foot in front of you until the last possible moment before moving it back. (For fuller details of the carriage of weight, see the chapter on Balance.) Each walk takes one beat of the music and is counted "slow". Repeat with the opposite leg.

When you are fairly proficient, endeavour to curve your walking steps inwards—slightly towards the middle of the floor. This will make you step into a contrary body movement position whenever you step back with the R.F. In other words, lock your thighs when you step back with the R.F. and unlock them when you step back with the L.F.

This latter "locking and unlocking" should be applied to every normal step backward in the Tango, where your partner is in front of you: it does not apply in outside or promenade figures.

The Progressive Side Step

GENTLEMAN

1. Step forward and across slightly to the R. with the
   L.F.   Q.
2. Short step to the side and slightly back with the
   R.F.   Q.
3. Step forward and across slightly to the R. with the
   L.F.   S.

Contrary body movement position. Used on 1 and 3.

LADY

1. Step back and across slightly to the L. with the
   R.F.   Q.
2. Short step to the side and slightly forward with
   the L.F.   Q.
3. Step back and across slightly to the L. with the
   R.F.   S.

Contrary body movement position. Used on 1 and 3.

THE PROGRESSIVE SIDE STEP

GENTLEMAN

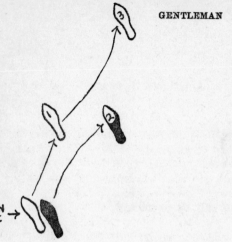

BEGIN HERE →

LADY

BEGIN HERE →

The Basic Reverse Turn

GENTLEMAN

1. Step forward with the L.F. turning on it to the L.   Q.
2. Short step to the side with the R.F. still turning.   Q.
3. Cross the L.F. over in front of the R.F.   S.
4. Step back with the R.F. turning on it to the L.   Q.
5. Short step to the side with the L.F.   Q.
6. Close the R.F. up to the L.F.   S.

Contrary body movement position. Used on 1 and 4.

NOTE.—On the first three steps make a third of a turn. On the last three steps make a quarter turn as described, or make no turn at all.

THE REVERSE TURN

GENTLEMAN

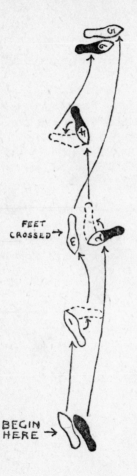

The Basic Reverse Turn

LADY

1. Step back with the R.F. turning on it to the L.   Q.
2. Very short step to the side with the L.F.   Q.
3. Close the R.F. up to the L.F.   S.
4. Step forward with the L.F. turning on it to the L.   Q.
5. Small step to the side with the R.F.   Q.
6. Close the L.F. up to the R.F.   S.

Contrary body movement position. Used on 1 and 4.

NOTE.—On the first three steps make a third of a turn. On the last three steps make a quarter turn as described, or make no turn at all.

THE REVERSE TURN

LADY

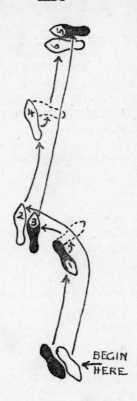

BEGIN
HERE

THE CLOSED PROMENADE

This figure is taken sideways to the line of dance.

GENTLEMAN

1. Step to side with the L.F. in P.P.   S.
2. Step through with the R.F. in P.P.   Q.
3. Short step to the side with the L.F.   Q.
4. Close the R.F. up to the L.F.   S.

Contrary body movement position. Used on 2.

LADY

1. Step to side with the R.F. in P.P.   S.
2. Step through with the L.F. in P.P.   Q.
3. Short step to the side with the R.F.   Q.
4. Close the L.F. up to the R.F.   S.

Contrary body movement position. Used on 2.

The Closed Promenade

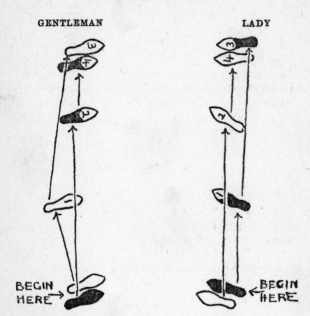

The Back Corté

GENTLEMAN

1. Step back with the L.F.   S.
2. Step back with the R.F. turning very slightly to the L.   Q.
3. Small step to the side with the L.F.   Q.
4. Close the R.F. up to the L.F.   S.

Contrary body movement. Used on 2.

LADY

1. Step forward with the R.F.   S.
2. Step forward with the L.F. turning very slightly to the L. Q.
3. Small step to the side with the R.F.   Q.
4. Close the L.F. up to the R.F.   S.

Contrary body movement. Used on 2.

The Back Corté

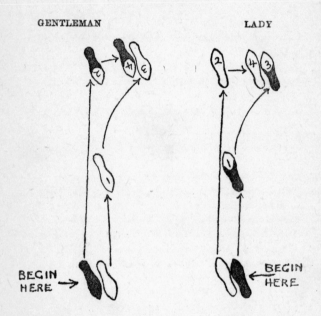

THE NATURAL TURN

(also known as the NATURAL TWIST TURN)

Begin this figure sideways to the line of dance.

GENTLEMAN

1. Step to side with the L.F. in P.P.   S.
2. Step through with the R.F. in P.P. turning on it to
       the R.   Q.
3. Step to the side with the L.F. still turning.   Q.
4. Cross the R.F. behind the L.F. with feet apart
       (back to L.O.D.).   S.
5. } Swivel three-quarters of a turn to the R. (on
6. }   L. heel and ball of R.F.) finishing with weight on
       the R.F. (finish with feet closed together).   Q.Q.
       After this go straight into the Closed Promenade,
       or the Back Corté.

Contrary body movement position. Used on 2.

THE NATURAL TURN

(also known as the NATURAL TWIST TURN)

LADY

1. Step to side with the R.F. in P.P.   S.
2. Step through with the L.F. in P.P.   Q.
3. Step forward with the R.F.   Q.
4. Step forward with the L.F. preparing to step outside partner.   S.
5. Step forward with the R.F. outside partner turning on it to the R.   Q.
6. Close the L.F. up to the R.F. still turning.   Q.
    After this go straight into the Closed Promenade, or the Back Corté.

Contrary body movement position. Used on 2 and 5.

THE OPEN REVERSE TURN

This figure can be used in two or three different ways. The best way is to do 1, 2, 3, (described below) and then finish with 4, 5, 6, of the Basic Reverse Turn.

GENTLEMAN

1. Step forward with the L.F. turning on it to the L.   Q.
2. Step to the side with the R.F. still turning.   Q.
3. Step back with the L.F. (or leading partner outside).   S.
4. Step back with the R.F. turning on it to the L.   Q.
5. Very short step to the side with the L.F.   Q.
6. Step forward with the R.F. (or outside partner).   S.

Contrary body movement position. Used on 1, 4. (If partner is outside then C.B.M.P. is used on 1, 3, 4, 6.)

LADY

1. Step back with the R.F. turning on it to the L.   Q.
2. Close the L.F. back to the R.F. turning from R. heel on to L. heel (heel turn—feet slightly apart).   Q.
3. Step forward with the R.F. (or outside partner).   S.
4. Step forward with the L.F. turning on it to the L.   Q.
5. Step to the side with the R.F.   Q.
6. Step back with the L.F. (or partner outside).   S.

Contrary body movement position. Used on 1, 4. (If your partner leads you outside him, then C.B.M.P. is used on 1, 3, 4, 6.)

The Open Promenade

Begin this figure sideways to the line of dance.

GENTLEMAN

Do 1, 2, of the Closed Promenade.		S.Q.
3.	Short step to the side with the L.F.	Q.
4.	Step forward with the R.F. outside partner.	S.

After this go straight into the Progressive Side Step.

Contrary body movement position. Used on 2 and 4.

LADY

Do 1, 2, of the Closed Promenade.		S.Q.
3.	Short step to the side with the R.F.	Q.
4.	Step back with the L.F. (your partner steps outside).	S.

After this go straight into the Progressive Step.

Contrary body movement position. Used on 2 and 4.

NATURAL PROMENADE TURN

Begin this figure facing the outside of the room—the wall. Make a complete turn in this figure or if used on a corner three-quarters of a turn.

GENTLEMAN

1. Step to side with the L.F. in P.P.   S.
2. Step through with the R.F. in P.P. turning on it
   to the R.   Q.
3. Step to the side with the L.F. still turning.   Q.
4. Step forward on to the R.F. still turning.   S.
   Then go straight into the Closed Promenade.

Contrary body movement. Used on 2 and 4

THE ROCK (No. 2)

This figure may be used when the gentleman is in a position to go backwards with his R.F.

GENTLEMAN

1. Step back with the R.F. preparing to rock.   Q.
2. Rock forward on to the L.F.   Q.
3. Rock back on to the R.F.   S.
   There are one or two alternative endings. The most usual is to go straight into the Back Corté.

Contrary body movement position. Retained throughout on 1, 2 and 3.

LADY

1. Step forward with the L.F. preparing to rock.   Q.
2. Rock back on to the R.F.   Q.
3. Rock forward on to the L.F.   S.

Contrary body movement position. Retained throughout on 1, 2 and 3.

The Rock Turn

GENTLEMAN

1. Step forward with the R.F. turning on it to the R.   S.
2. Step to the side with the L.F. preparing to rock.   Q.
3. Rock forward on to the R.F. still turning slightly.   Q.
4. Rock back on to the L.F.   S.
5, 6, 7. Then go straight into 4, 5, 6, of the Basic Reverse Turn.

Contrary body movement. Used slightly on 1 and 5.

LADY

1. Step back with the L.F. turning on it to the R.   S.
2. Step to the side with the R.F. preparing to rock.   Q.
3. Rock back on to the L.F. still turning slightly.   Q.
4. Rock forward on to the R.F.   S.
5, 6, 7. Then go straight into 4, 5, 6, of the Basic Reverse Turn.

Contrary body movement. Used slightly on 1 and 5.

The Progressive Side Step Reverse Turn

GENTLEMAN

1. Step forward and across slightly to the R. with the L.F. turning on it to the L.   Q.
2. Small step to the side with the R.F. still turning.   Q.
3. Step forward and across slightly to the R. with the L.F.   S.
4. Step forward with the R.F.   S.
5. Step back with the L.F. (ready to rock).   Q.
6. Rock forward on to the R.F.   Q.
7. Rock back on to the L.F.   S.
8. Step back with the R.F. turning on it to the L.   S.
9. After this go straight into   Q.
10. the Progressive Side Step   Q.
11. turning on it to face the L.O.D.   S.
    Another alternative ending is—after No. 7, go into 4, 5, 6, of the Basic Reverse Turn.

Contrary body movement position. Used on 1, 3, 8, 9, 11.

The Progressive Side Step Reverse Turn

LADY

1. Step back and across slightly to the L. with the R.F. turning on it to the L.   Q.
2. Small step to the side with the L.F. still turning.   Q.
3. Step back and across slightly to the L. with the R.F.   S.
4. Step back with the L.F.   S.
5. Step forward with the R.F. (ready to rock).   Q.
6. Rock back on to the L.F.   Q.
7. Rock forward on to the R.F.   S.
8. Step forward with the L.F. turning on it to the L.   S.
9. { After this go straight into   Q.
10. { the Progressive Side Step   Q.
11. { turning on it so that you finish with your back to the L.O.D.   S.

   Another alternative ending is—after No. 7, go into 4, 5, 6, of the Basic Reverse Turn.

Contrary body movement position. Used on 1, 3, 8, 9, 11.

How to Construct the Tango

Avoid using walking steps in between the different figures as much as possible. At the most never use more than two walking steps at a time.

After the Progressive Side Step do one walk forward on the R.F., and then go into a reverse turn, or, make a quarter turn to the R. on the R.F. and go into one of the promenades.

After a reverse turn (which has finished with the feet closed together) go into a promenade if you are sideways to the line of dance, or into a Back Corté if you have your back to the line of dance.

After a Closed Promenade go straight into the Progressive Side Step, or follow it with an Open Promenade, or a Natural Turn. If you are near the end of the room—the corner—go straight into a Back Corté.

After a Back Corté, if you turn slightly on the second step, you will be in the correct position to go into a promenade.

After a Natural Turn go straight into a promenade or a Back Corté.

The figures can be mixed up in many different ways. According to a dancer's ability and experience, so he can add other figures, but it is much better to make sure of these standardized figures and amalgamating them before attempting anything more advanced.

THE CUBAN RUMBA

RUMBAS are played quite frequently in many ballrooms to-day and as a consequence of this the Ballroom Committee of the Imperial Society have standardized the figures described below.

The hold differs from other dances in that the man holds his partner about eighteen inches away from him. The lady should lean back slightly so that she is supported by her partner's right hand. He gives the indication for every figure that he wishes to lead with this hand. There is no rise and fall in the figures described below.

The majority of figures are timed S.Q.Q. but owing to a subtlety in the rhythm dancers will get the finished way of performing them by *thinking* of the steps as S.S.Q. This means that the second step (Q.) must be taken a fraction slower, and the third step (Q.) a fraction quicker. The true steps must of course, be fitted to four beats of the music. The descriptions are of the gentleman's steps, the lady's being the opposite unless otherwise mentioned.

THE SQUARE (RIGHT)

This figure is taken forwards and backwards in the same place.

1. Step forward with R.F.   S.
2. Short step to side with L.F.   Q.
3. Close R.F. up to L.F. relaxing knees slightly.   Q.
4. Step back with L.F.   S.
5. Short step to side with R.F.   Q.
6. Close L.F. up to R.F. relaxing knees slightly.   Q.
   Repeat *ad. lib.*

The lady does 4, 5, 6, whilst the man does 1, 2, 3, and vice-versa.

THE SQUARE DESCRIBED ABOVE IS USED AS A NATURAL TURN.

Turn slightly to the R. on 1 and 4. This turn is non-progressive. You should take about 3 squares turning, to make one full turn.

THE SQUARE (LEFT)

This figure is taken forwards and backwards in the same place.

1. Step forward with L.F.   S.
2. Short step to side with R.F.   Q.
3. Close L.F. up to R.F. relaxing knees slightly.   Q.
4. Step back with R.F.   S.
5. Short step to side with L.F.   Q.
6. Close R.F. up to L.F. relaxing knees slightly.   Q.

The lady does 4, 5, 6, whilst the man does 1, 2, 3, and vice-versa.

The Square Described Above is Used as a Reverse Turn.

Turn slightly to the L. on 1 and 4. This turn is non-progressive. You should take about 3 squares turning, to make one full turn.

The Half Square (forwards)

1.	Step forward with R.F.	S.
2.	Short step to side with L.F.	Q.
3.	Close R.F. up to L.F. relaxing knees slightly.	Q.
4.	Step forward with L.F.	S.
5.	Short step to side with R.F.	Q.
6.	Close L.F. up to R.F. relaxing knees slightly.	Q.

The Half Square (backwards)

1.	Step back with L.F.	S.
2.	Short step to side with R.F.	Q.
3.	Close L.F. up to R.F. relaxing knees slightly.	Q.
4.	Step back with R.F.	S.
5.	Short step to side with L.F.	Q.
6.	Close R.F. up to L.F. relaxing knees slightly.	Q.

Whilst the gentleman is doing the Half Square forwards, the lady is doing the Half Square backwards and vice versa.

THE WALK

To go into this figure, in which the man usually progresses backwards, do so after No. 3 on the Right Square turning, when the man has his back to the L.O.D. It may also be used after No. 3 of the Left Square in which case the man would begin the Walk, described below, with his R.F.

1. Step back with L.F. (knee straight).   Q.
2. Bring R.F. close to L.F. keeping weight on L.F. (relaxing knees).   Q.
3. Short step to side with R.F. keeping weight on L.F. (straightening L. knee).   Q.
4. Bring R.F. close to L.F. keeping weight on L.F. (relaxing knees).   Q.
   Repeat, starting back with R.F.

To come out of this figure after No. 4, do so by stepping forward with the R.F. into the Right Square, or conversely with the L.F. into the Left Square.

THE PROGRESSIVE STEP

To go into this figure, in which the man usually progresses backwards, do so after No. 3 of the Right Square turning, when the man has his back to the L.O.D. It may also be used after No. 3 of the Left Square in which case the man would begin the Progressive Step with his R.F.

1. Short step back with L.F. and immediately kick R.F. forward very slightly, relaxing L. knee.   S.
2. Short step back with R.F.   Q.
3. Short step back with L.F.   Q.
   Repeat, starting back with R.F.

To come out of this figure after No. 3, do so by stepping back with the R.F. into 5, 6, of the Left Square, or conversely with the L.F. into 5, 6, of the Right Square.

THE TURNS (CUBAN TOP)

In the turns the lady and gentleman move round in a circle which has for an axis a point half way between the two dancers. Both the lady and gentleman use a succession of side and cross steps; when one crosses the other steps to the side and vice versa. For general teaching purposes it is easier to teach the man to mark time whilst his partner does the stepping to the side and the crossing. The turns are done to the right and the left (natural and reverse). To go into the turns do so as follows:—Do 1, 2, 3, 4, of the Right Square, S.Q.Q.S., then:—

GENTLEMAN

Cross R.F. behind L.F.	Q.
Side L.F.	Q.
Cross R.F. in front or behind L.F.	S.
Side L.F.	Q.
Cross R.F. in front or behind L.F.	Q.
Side L.F.	S.
Cross R.F. in front or behind L.F.	Q.
Side L.F.	Q.
Close R.F. to L.F.	S,

At this point the man stops his turn to the right and commences to turn to left, as follows:—

Cross L.F. behind R.F.	Q.
Side R.F.	Q.
Cross L.F. behind or in front of R.F.	S.
Side R.F.	Q.
Cross L.F. behind or in front of R.F.	Q.
Side R.F.	S.
Cross L.F. behind R.F.	Q.
Side R.F.	Q.
Forward L.	S.

—into 2, 3, of the Left Square.

Do 1, 2, 3, 4, of the Right Square, S.Q.Q.S., then:—

Side L.F.	Q.
Cross R.F. in front of L.F.	Q.
Side L.F.	S.
Cross R.F. in front or behind L.F.	Q.
Side L.F.	Q.
Cross R.F. in front or behind L.F.	S.
Side L.F.	Q.
Cross R.F. in front or behind L.F.	Q.
Side L.F.	S.

At this point the lady stops her turn to the right and begins to turn to the left, as follows:—

Side R.F.	Q.
Cross L.F. in front of R.F.	Q.
Side R.F.	S.
Cross L.F. in front or behind R.F.	Q.
Side R.F.	Q.
Cross L.F. in front or behind R.F.	S.
Side R.F.	Q.
Cross L.F. in front of R.F.	Q.
Back R.F. into 5, 6, of the Left Square.	S.

RHYTHM DANCING

WHAT is Rhythm Dancing?
It is the new technique for crowded floors. And so many floors are crowded nowadays that Rhythm Dancing is a necessity.

It is one of those tendencies which forces itself into prominence. Circumstances are all in favour of it, so long as people are really keen on dancing.

It becomes more and more difficult to dance the standard dances in many of the smaller resorts, as the number of would-be dancers seem to increase almost daily.

There have been previous attempts to deal with the situation. You will have heard of Crush Dancing, which has been the answer so far to the question: "What can I dance in a crowd?"

Crush Dancing, as it has been called in the past, was not a good name—too reminiscent of a tube train in the rush hours. And it was not a fully developed technique. But it served a purpose.

Recently the Ballroom Committee of the Imperial Society of Teachers of Dancing decided that the time had come to standardize it. The first move was to change the name, and it was resolved unanimously to call it Rhythm Dancing in place of the unattractive name which it had held heretofore. The new name is a very good description of it. The essence of rhythm dancing is a condenzation of the orthodox dances.

Steps are telescoped, elaborate spins and pivots are cut out altogether, outside steps are reduced to a minimum, and a number of non-progressive figures are introduced. Contrary body movement is drastically reduced. Rise and fall almost disappears.

It is not necessary to change the ordinary ballroom hold, but there is a tendency to make it more compact—for the man to place his right hand a little farther round his partner, and to bend his left elbow more sharply.

Rhythm Dancing is chiefly important for 4/4 music played at any tempo. Tango, in its more finished form, is already almost a "crush" dance in comparison with the others, as it has no rise and fall, and many of its figures require little space. It is just a question of slightly shortening the stride and avoiding anything complicated. Also many dancers are shy of attempting a Tango, and it is, therefore, not so liable to be crowded out.

The chief thing to remember about the Waltz is to shorten your steps, then the ordinary Natural and Reverse Turns and the Changes take up very little space. When necessary you can introduce hesitations—step out on the first beat of the bar and pause for the second and third beats.

Reverting to 4/4 music, the Ballroom Committee standardized Rhythm Dancing in two forms—Slow and Quick.

Quick Rhythm Dancing can be used to all 4/4 music played at a tempo that is faster than approximately 38 bars to the minute. The Slow form would, of course, be used to any tempo slower than that.

The descriptions are of the gentleman's steps, the lady's being the opposite unless otherwise mentioned.

QUICK RHYTHM DANCING

THE WALK

This consists of a series of short steps which are taken with a slight lilting movement. The lilt is obtained by relaxing the back knee slightly and gradually as the other foot moves forward. The relaxing of the knee must be a soft movement, not a sharp jerky one.

Each walk is a slow step and takes 2 beats of the music. The walk backwards—the opposite.

THE QUARTER TURNS

This figure is similar to the standard figure of that name in the Quickstep. All rise and fall should be eliminated unless space permits, and every step should be a short one. The chassé on 2, 3, 4, should be an open one. The man should take the heel pivot on 6, 7, with his L.F. a few inches in advance of his R.F. A quarter turn to the R. should be made between steps 1 to 4, and another quarter turn to the L. between steps 5 to 8.

Begin facing diagonally to wall.

1.	Short step forward with R.F. turning on it to R.	S.
2.	Short step to side with L.F. still turning.	Q.
3.	Half close R.F. to L.F.	Q.
4.	Short step diagonally back with L.F.	S.
5.	Short step back with R.F., turning on it to L.	S.
6.	Close L.F. back to R.F. keeping L.F. a few inches	
7.	in advance (of R.F.) whilst turning to L. on R. heel	Q.Q.
8.	Short step forward with L.F.	S.

NOTE.—On 6 the lady should take a short step to side with R.F., and on 7 she should half close her L.F. to R.F. (an open chassé).

The same lilting movement as described above for the Walk, should be used in this figure.

The Natural Pivot Turn

1. Short step forward with R.F., turning on it to R. S.
2. Short step to side with L.F. still turning. Q.
3. Half close R.F. to L.F. Q.
4. Short step diagonally back with L.F., turning slightly to R. S.

Repeat two or three times in order to make one full turn.

The Chassé Reverse Turn

This figure is similar to the standard figure of that name in the Quickstep. All rise and fall should be eliminated unless space permits, and every step should be a short one. Instead of making just over three-quarters of a turn on the complete figure as in the Quickstep, the figure should be repeated two or three times in order to make one full turn. The heel pivot on 5, 6, should be taken in the same way as described for the Quarter Turns. The chassé on 2, 3, 4, should be an open one.

1. Short step forward with L.F. turning on it to L. S.
2. Short step to side with R.F. still turning Q.
3. Half close L.F. to R.F. Q.
4. Short step back with R.F. turning on it to L. S.
5. ⎰ Close L.F. back to R.F., keeping L.F. a few inches
6. ⎱   in advance (of R.F.) whilst turning to L. on
       R. heel Q.Q.
7. Short step forward with L.F. S.

Note.—On 5 the lady should take a short step to side with R.F. and on 6 she should half close her L.F. to R.F. (an open chassé).

The man's step on 3, 4, is a heel pivot as in Quarter Turns.

THE REVERSE PIVOT TURN

1.   Short step forward with L.F., pivoting on it slightly
     to L.   S.
2.   Balance back on to R.F. still turning to L.   S.
3. ⎧ Close L.F. back to R.F. keeping L.F. a few inches
4. ⎨   in advance (of R.F.) whilst turning to L. on R.
     ⎩   heel   Q.Q.
Repeat two or three times in order to make one full turn.

NOTE.—On 3 the lady should take a short step to side
with R.F. and on 4 she should half close her L.F. to R.F.
(an open chassé).

The man's step on 3, 4, is a heel pivot as in Quarter Turns.

THE BACK CORTÉ

1.   Short step back with R.F. turning on it slightly
     to L.   S.
2. ⎧ Close L.F. back to R.F. keeping L.F. a few inches
3. ⎨   in advance (of R.F.) whilst turning slightly to
     ⎩   L. on R. heel   Q.Q.
4.   Short step back with L.F.   S.
Repeat *ad. lib.*
NOTE.—On 2 the lady should take a short step to side
with R.F. and on 3 she should half close her L.F. to R.F.
(an open chassé).

THE CHANGE OF DIRECTION

This figure is similar to the standard figure of that name
in the Quickstep.

1.   Short step diagonally forward on to inside of R.F.   S.
2.   Brush L.F. up to R.F. turning to L. on R.F.
        (relaxing knees)   S.
3.   Short step forward with L.F.   S.

THE SIDE STEP

This figure is taken sideways to the line of dance, the gentleman facing the wall throughout.

1. Short step to side with L.F.   Q.
2. Half close R.F. to L.F.   Q.
3. Step to the side again with L.F.   S.
4. Close R.F. up to L.F.   S.
    Repeat *ad. lib.*

SLOW RHYTHM DANCING

THE WALK

This consists of a series of steps which are taken with a slight lilting movement. The length is decided by the space available. If possible the steps should be of natural length. The lilt is obtained by relaxing the back knee slightly and gradually, as the other foot moves forward. The relaxing of the knee must be a soft movement—not a sharp jerky one.

Each walk is a slow step and takes two beats of the music. The walk backwards—the opposite.

THE CHASSÉS

On all chassés, if space permits, rise at the end of the first quick step, and lower at the end of the second quick step.

SIDE CHASSÉ ON RIGHT FOOT

	1.	Walk forward on L.F., using C.B.M.	S.
Chassé	2.	Step to side with R.F.	Q.
	3.	Close L.F. to R.F.	Q.
	4.	Step to side again with R.F.	S.
	5.	Brush L.F. through (close to R.F.) and step forward with it	S.

NOTE.—In the Chassé (Nos. 2, 3, 4) the man travels sideways diagonally to the wall, which means to say that he faces diagonally to centre. The C.B.M. on 1 will bring him into this position.

NOTE.—The same lilting movement as described for the Walk should be used on the slow steps in this figure.

Quarter Turns

This figure is similar to the standard figure of that name
in the Quickstep.

A quarter turn to the R. should be made between steps
1 to 4, and another quarter turn to the L. between steps
5 to 8.

Begin facing diagonally to the wall.

	1.	Step forward with R.F., turning on it to the R.	S.
Chassé {	2.	Step to side with L.F. still turning	Q.
	3.	Close R.F. to L.F.	Q.
	4.	Step diagonally back with L.F.	S.
	5.	Step back with R.F. turning on it to L.	S.
Chassé {	6.	Short step to side with L.F.	Q.
	7.	Close R.F. to L.F.	Q.
	8.	Step forward with L.F.	S.

Note.—The same lilting movement as described for the
Walk should be used on the slow steps in this figure.

The Natural Pivot Turn

	1.	Step forward with R.F. turning on it to R.	S.
Chassé {	2.	Step to side with L.F. still turning	Q.
	3.	Close R.F. to L.F.	Q.
	4.	Step diagonally back with L.F. still turning slightly to the R.	S.

Repeat two or three times in order to make one full turn.

Note.—The same lilting movement as described for the
Walk should be used on the slow steps in this figure.

The Chassé Reverse Turn

This figure is similar to the standard figure of that name in the Quickstep.

	1.	Step forward with L.F. turning on it to L.	S.
Chassé	2.	Step to side with R.F. still turning	Q.
	3.	Close L.F. to R.F.	Q.
	4.	Step back with R.F. turning on it to L.	S.
Chassé	5.	Short step to side with L.F.	Q.
	6.	Close R.F. to L.F.	Q.
	7.	Step forward with L.F.	S.

Note.—The same lilting movement as described for the Walk should be used on the slow steps in this figure.

The Back Corté

This figure is taken with the man travelling in a backward direction throughout.

1.	Step back with R.F. turning on it slightly to L.	S.
2.	Short step to side with L.F.	Q.
3.	Close R.F. to L.F.	Q.
4.	Step diagonally back with L.F. turning very slightly to R.	S.
	Repeat *ad. lib.*	

Note.—The same lilting movement as described for the Walk should be used on the slow steps in this figure.

THE SIDE STEP

This figure is taken sideways to the line of dance, the gentleman facing the wall throughout.

Open Chassé
1.	Step to side with L.F.		Q.
2.	Half close R.F. to L.F.		Q.
3.	Step to side again with L.F.		S.
4.	Balance back on to R.F. (which is to the side)		S.

Repeat *ad. lib.*

The same lilting movement as described for the Walk should be used on the slow steps in this figure.

SEQUENCE DANCES

These dances (described in the following pages) differ from the standard ballroom dances in that every dancer does the same steps at the same time. These sequence or party dances are really *romping* rather than *dancing,* but they are featured in the majority of ballrooms to-day.

THE LAMBETH WALK

A 16 bar sequence dance in 4/4 time. Tempo 44 bars per minute. There are four figures, each taking four bars. Music "The Lambeth Walk." Record No.—Parlophone. F1115.

1. THE WALK. 4 *bars.* Man inside of room, lady outside. Both facing L.O.D. Man begins L.F., lady R.F. Do 8 Lambeth Walks forward along the room. Swing arms while walking.

2. THE CIRCLES. 4 *bars.* Link L. arms. Man begins L.F., lady R.F. Do four walks forward in circle making half turn to L., then about turn and, linking R. arms, do four walks forward in circle making half turn to R. and finish facing L.O.D.

3. THE ROCKS. 4 *bars.* Lady links L. arm in gentleman's R. Man begins L.F., lady R.F. Do 3 walks forward counting it S.S.Q. Rock back on to R.F. Q. Rock forward on to L.F. S.
Repeat above—man beginning R.F., lady L.F.

S.S.Q.Q.S.

4. THE PROMENADE. 4 *bars.* Man begins L.F., lady R.F. Both facing L.O.D. The man takes 3 walks towards middle of room, the lady taking 3 walks towards wall. Join R.F. to L.F. (lady L.F. to R.F.) and both turning to face partner, at same time slapping knees, then:—
Do 3 Lambeth Walks towards each other and join R.F. to L.F. (lady L.F. to R.F.) turning to face L.O.D., at same time raising thumb and shouting "Oi."
Repeat *ad lib.*

THE BLACK-OUT STROLL

Reproduced by kind permission of Frances Day & Hunter, who publish the music for the dance. This dance is recorded by Victor Silvester and his Ballroom Orchestra on Parlophone F1595.

Partners hold in the normal dancing position for Figures 1 and 2. The gentleman's steps only are described, the lady's being the opposite.

FIRST FIGURE: THE STROLL

Beginning on left foot walk four steps forward on alternate feet.

(Left (*S*) Right (*S*) Left (*S*) Right (*S*))

SECOND FIGURE: THE FORWARD CHASSÉ

Left foot forward and to side. Close right foot to left, left foot forward and to side.

(Left (*Q*) Right (*Q*) Left (*S*))

Repeat, beginning on right foot, lady turning clockwise into 'side by side' position holding inside hands.

(Right (*Q*) Left (*Q*) Right (*S*))

THIRD FIGURE: THE BREAK

Chassé away from each other. Left foot to side, close right foot to left, left foot to side.

(Left (*Q*) Right (*Q*) Left (*S*))

Chassé back to place. Right foot to side, close left foot to right, right foot to side.

(Right (Q) Left (Q) Right (S))

FOURTH FIGURE: THE ROMP

Turning to face each other, gentleman holds partner to his right side, his right round waist, her right hand on his left and romping round each other one complete turn counting, one, two, three, hop.

Left foot forward.

Right foot forward.

Left foot forward and hop.

Repeat, beginning on right foot and finish opposite each other.

Gentlemen change partners on end of Chorus as lights are lowered. Lights up again at beginning of next Chorus.

"KNEES UP MOTHER BROWN"

(The 5th of C. L. Heimann's Novelty Dances)
Reproduced by kind permission of the Peter Maurice Music Co., who publish the music for the dance. The Ballroom Routine was devised by Adele England.

Partners hold in the normal dancing position for the verse and facing each other for the chorus.

Steps described are gentlemen's, lady commences on the opposite foot.

VERSE:

Commencing on the L.F., The One Step. 8 Walking steps forward, moving the left arm backwards and forwards as you walk.

One complete turn to the right, taking 8 beats, balancing from one foot to the other—swaying the shoulders from side to side as you turn.

Now repeat the above figure, 8 One Steps and 1 complete turn, finish facing each other and shout "ooh."

CHORUS:

Facing each other, commence on the R.F. 3 Running steps forward, on the 4th beat slip forward with bended knees—shouting "Well," slightly lifting trousers while lady slightly lifts dress.

Then 4 running steps back to places still facing each other.

Hop on the R.F. twice, at the same time extend right hand slightly lowered towards partner, palm upwards, keeping in time with each Hop. Repeat on the L.F. and left hand. Again on the right and again on the left.

Commence on R.F. Running towards partner link right arms, make a circle, and back to places.

Hopping on one foot then the other with the knees up. 4 Facing each other and 4 moving towards each other, finishing with the shout "ooh."

Now repeat the Verse, and Chorus as many times as desired.

"BOOMPS-A-DAISY"

Reproduced by kind permission of the Lawrence Wright Music Co., Ltd., who publish the music for the dance. Recorded by Victor Silvester and his Ballroom Orchestra on Parlophone, F1461.

"Boomps-a-Daisy" is arranged in a 16 bars sequence and is danced as follows:—

1st Bar

Partners stand facing each other, gentleman facing wall. On the first beat of the bar they clap each others hands (gent's R.H. claps against lady's L. and vice versa) as they clap they shout "HANDS!"

2nd Bar

In the same position as above, partners slap their own knees on the first beat of the bar shouting "KNEES!"

3RD BAR

Turning about ¼ turn to left the gentleman 'bumps' his right hip against the lady's left hip. The lady has turned about ¼ turn to right, as they 'bump' on the first beat of the bar they shout "BOOMPS!" and on the third beat they shout "A"

4TH BAR

Turning back to the original position, the lady and gentleman bow to each other, shouting "DAI" on the first beat and "SY" on the third beat of the bar.

5TH BAR

The gentleman steps to the side on the left foot on the first beat of the bar. On the second and third beats he swings his right leg across his left. The lady, facing gentleman, does corresponding movements, stepping to the side with the right foot and swinging left leg.

6TH BAR

The gentleman steps to the side on the right foot on the first beat of the bar. On the second and third beats he swings his left leg across his right. The lady, facing gentleman, does corresponding movements, stepping to the side with the left foot and swinging right leg.

7TH AND 8TH BARS

Gentleman commencing forward with left foot in line of dance on the first beat of the 7th bar, dances 6 steps of reverse waltz on his own, finishing facing his partner. Lady dances 6 steps of natural waltz turn commencing forward with right foot in line of dance, finishing facing partner. At the end of the 8th bar the lady and gentleman should stand facing each other as in starting position (beginning of 1st bar).

9TH, 10TH, 11TH AND 12TH BARS

Repeat 1st, 2nd, 3rd and 4th Bars.

13TH, 14TH, 15TH AND 16TH BARS

Lady and gentleman dance four bars of old-fashioned waltz natural turns.

NOTE: The gentleman should begin his old-fashioned waltz with the LEFT foot.

THE PALAIS GLIDE

THE Palais Glide is danced in groups of from 2 to 8 (or even more) people extended in line, facing the line of dance with their arms linked round each other's waists.

The dance is arranged to an 8-bar sequence in 4/4 time, and everyone begins with the left foot. It is very simple.

1. Point L. heel diagonally forward (heel on floor, toe in the air), weight on R.F.   S.
2. Step back with L.F. behind R.F.   Q.
3. Short step to side with R.F.   Q.
4. Step forward and across with L.F. in front of R.F.   S.
5. Point R. heel diagonally forward (heel on floor, toe in the air), weight on L.F.   S.
6. Step back with R.F. behind L.F.   Q.
7. Short step to side with L.F.   Q.
8. Step forward and across with R.F. in front of L.F.   S.
9. Point L. heel diagonally forward (heel on floor, toe in the air), weight on R.F.   S.
10. Step back with L.F. behind R.F.   Q.
11. Short step to side with R.F.   Q.
12. Swing L.F. forward and cross it over in front of R.F.   S.
13. Swing R.F. forward and cross it over in front of L.F.   S.
14. Swing L.F. forward and cross it over in front of R.F.   S.

15. Swing R.F. forward and cross it over in front of L.F.   S.
16. Step forward with L.F.   Q.
17. Swing R.F. forward, keeping weight on L.F.   Q.
18. Swing R.F. back, keeping weight on L.F. and leaning forward   S.
19. Step forward with R.F.   Q.
20. Very short step forward with L.F.   Q.
21. Very short step forward with R.F.   S.

Repeat the entire sequence *ad lib.*

THEORY AND TECHNIQUE OF BALLROOM DANCING

by Victor Silvester

Crown Octavo   *3s. 6d. net*

This book covers everything that is essential in connection with Ballroom Dancing, from a detailed description of the standardized figures down to the finer points which proclaim the expert dancer. A complete syllabus for a Ballroom Examination is given together with two hundred and thirty-one questions and answers, and a complete analysis of the fundamental principles and everything that it is necessary to know from the viewpoint of the experienced performer. In short, here is a book that is absolutely indispensable both to the novice and to the experienced or professional performer.

TAP-DANCING AT A GLANCE

by Jimmy Ormonde

With 150 Illustrations. Crown Octavo   *2s. net*

Tap-dancing is not really so difficult—you can learn easily if you follow these simple instructions. Through the use of posed photographs the author has analysed the movements so that those who have never danced before can learn in their own homes to become as proficient in this type of dancing as those who have spent great sums of money in dancing schools. Practise the steps patiently, and you will be amazed at your progress within a month or two.

ENQUIRE WITHIN UPON EVERYTHING

119TH EDITION

2s. 6d. *net*

Enquire Within has an answer for every question you put to it. It will enable you to cure a cold, plan a dinner, make a will or get married. It will assist you to serve dainty dishes, play games and clean soiled paint. It will advise you in your relations with your landlord, assist you in curing simple ailments and guide you upon difficult points of etiquette. Enquirers on the Laws of Husband and Wife, Debtor and Creditor, Employer and Employed, Health Insurance, Pensions, Rent Restriction Acts, Wills and Intestacy, are supplied with the latest information.

Whatever you may wish to do, make, learn to enjoy, *Enquire Within* will never fail you. In many cases you will find that it takes the place of the Lawyer and the Doctor—and it can't send in a bill!

This edition has been carefully revised by experts, who have brought it completely up to date. But not only has the material been brought up-to-date but also the format of the book. Being printed in a better and clearer faced type, with a pleasing modern lay-out, it is easier to read and more attractive to handle. In fact, everything has been done to enhance the value of a work which is already prized by hundreds of readers.

THE CLOCK STRIKES TWELVE

by H. Russell Wakefield

7s. 6d. net

There is a singular lack of modern volumes of ghost stories. Possibly that is due to the fact that people find it difficult to thrill to the somewhat crude horrors, picturesque apparitions and blood-freezing groans which have been lavishly scattered in so many tales of the supernatural.

This volume is different because its effect of the macabre, its nerve-tensing atmosphere and its uncanny horror are contrived with greater subtlety. Only a reader completely devoid of imagination could fail to respond to its strange fascination.

H. Russell Wakefield is a master of this type of story. "An always successful and classically polished purveyor of horror," is how the *Observer* described him. There can be no question but that *The Clock Strikes Twelve* emphatically justifies that description.

"Has authentic flavour . . . I recommend them strongly."
—*Observer*.

"Mr. Wakefield is a born writer of ghost stories. . . . There is at least one author able to write us, fluently and convincingly, into a state where insensate horror can touch the mind as lightly as an autumn leaf and leave a numb spot when it has passed."—*Truth*.

YOU AND YOUR STAR

A simplified system by which any person can find from his birthday the important years of his life, the illnesses or accidents likely to occur, the most favourable persons for marriage, unions, partnerships, etc., and his lucky days. No calculations are necessary as every day of any year is indicated.

15/- *net*

CHEIRO'S LANGUAGE OF THE HAND

This work has long been accepted as the classic of palmistry. It is a complete practical work on the Science of Cheirognomy and Cheiromancy, and contains, in addition to a large number of explanatory illustrations, thirty-two signed photogravure impressions of the hands of outstanding celebrities who have consulted Cheiro.

10/6 *net*

CHEIRO'S BOOK OF NUMBERS

A masterpiece of lucid teaching on the Science of Numerology, explaining the occult significance of numbers and their influence and relation to human life, and showing how to determine one's lucky or important numbers, the number value of one's name and propitious times for important transactions and decisions.

10/6 *net*